AMERICA'S DOWNTOWNS

GROWTH

POLITICS &

PRESERVATION

AMERICA'S DOWNTOWNS

GROWTH POLITICS & PRESERVATION

Richard C. Collins

Elizabeth B. Waters

A. Bruce Dotson

FOR THE NATIONAL TRUST
FOR HISTORIC PRESERVATION

Edited by
Constance Epton Beaumont

PRESERVATION PRESS

John Wiley & Sons, Inc.
New York Chichester Brisbane Toronto Singapore

The research for this book was made possible by a grant from the National Endowment for the Arts, the Henry M. Jackson Foundation, the Geraldine R. Dodge Foundation, the Mellon Bank of Pittsburgh and the John D. and Catherine T. MacArthur Foundation.

Printed in the United States of America
5 4 3 2

Library of Congress Cataloging in Publication Data
Collins, Richard C.
    America's downtowns : growth, politics, and preservation / Richard C. Collins, Elizabeth B. Waters, A. Bruce Dotson for the National Trust for Historic Preservation; edited by Constance Epton Beaumont.
        p. cm.
    ISBN 0-471-14499-1
    1. City planning—United States—Case studies. 2. Historic districts—United States—Conservation and restoration—Case studies. I. Waters, Elizabeth B. II. Dotson, Anthony Bruce. III. Beaumont, Constance Epton. IV. National Trust for Historic Preservation in the United States. V. Title.
HT167.C567 1990
307.1'216'0973—dc20   90-48661

Front cover: City of Paris building (1896), San Francisco, before its demolition in 1981. The building was lost in spite of a petition signed by 60,000 city residents urging the structure's preservation. The controversy surrounding the Beaux Arts building served as a catalyst for the city's Downtown Plan, enacted in 1985. The plan significantly strengthens protections for buildings such as the City of Paris. (© 1990 Craig Buchanan)

Back cover: Fountain Square, Cincinnati, a popular meeting place in this diverse city. A downtown plan calls for the highest height limits in the central core around Fountain Square.

Contents

Foreword

Historic preservation plays a central role in downtown revitalization. This book, *America's Downtowns: Growth, Politics and Preservation*, reports on an effort by the National Trust to assess the effectiveness of efforts in 10 cities to integrate preservation values into the local policies that shape downtown growth and development. But the reader might well ask, "Why is the National Trust interested in such urban affairs as growth management, planning and zoning?" After all, we are an organization that operates historic house museums, publishes a magazine featuring historic house restorations and assists owners of historic houses with their rehabilitation questions.

Local policies that shape urban growth and development are critical to the future of the American historic preservation movement and to that of America's cities. Chartered by Congress in 1949 to encourage public participation in the protection of the nation's cultural heritage, the National Trust sees it as an important part of its mission to encourage preservation-minded citizens to become involved in shaping the policies that shape cities.

We have a definite point of view on this subject. We believe that to become a great American city in the 21st century, a city must preserve those special places that make it a unique, interesting and attractive place to live and work. A city's historic landmarks and districts clearly rank prominently among such places.

Yet the preservation of these special places is too important to be left to chance; it requires planning as well as citizen involvement and constant vigilance. It is no coincidence that cities that make the lists of those places in which people want to live, visit as tourists and locate their businesses— for example, St. Paul, San Francisco and Seattle—have learned this lesson. Whether prodded by citizen initiatives or led by local officials, these cities are taking affirmative steps to retain their status as great American cities by preserving the best of their past.

For those cities interested in becoming better places in which to live and work, we offer eight specific recommendations. These recommendations, known as the Charleston Principles, were adopted unanimously by members of the national historic preservation community assembled on October 20, 1990, in Charleston, S.C., at the 44th annual conference of the National Trust. They are as follows:

- Identify historic places, both architectural and natural, that give the community its special character and that can aid its future well-being.

- Adopt the preservation of historic places as a goal of planning for land use, economic development, housing for all income levels and transportation.

- Create organizational, regulatory and incentive mechanisms to facilitate preservation and provide the leadership to make them work.

- Develop revitalization strategies that capitalize on the existing value of historic residential and commercial neighborhoods and properties and provide well-designed affordable housing without displacing existing residents.

- Ensure that policies and decisions on community growth and development respect a community's heritage and enhance overall livability.

- Demand excellence in design for new construction and in the stewardship of historic properties and places.

- Use a community's heritage to educate citizens of all ages and to build civic pride.

- Recognize the cultural diversity of communities and empower a diverse constituency to acknowledge, identify and preserve America's cultural and physical resources.

Failing to plan for and manage growth, or leaving the fate of cities to what Robert Campbell of the *Boston Globe* has called "the random collision of economic forces," is likely to result in the destruction of our historic places and in diminished cities.

We urge local preservation advocates to relate historic preservation to broader community concerns, including housing, economic development, tourism promotion and transportation. They can do this by explaining the contribution of preservation to their city's economy, by developing alliances with groups concerned with these other community issues and by joining forces with those concerned with a city's quality of life, including environmental and arts advocates, business leaders and the elderly, to name just a few.

Finally, we urge preservation leaders to look beyond traditional preservation ordinances and landmark commissions and to address those planning forums that have the most influence over their city's future development. Such forums include city councils, planning commissions, zoning and architectural review boards, economic development authorities and departments of public works. Preservation ordinances and commissions will remain vitally important, but their strength and potential usefulness can be undercut if preservation values are not reflected in local policies that set the stage for future development.

In publishing this book, the National Trust gratefully acknowledges the generous assistance received from the Design Arts Program of the National Endowment for the Arts, the Henry M. Jackson Foundation, the Geraldine R. Dodge Foundation, the John D. and Catherine T. MacArthur Foundation, and the Mellon Bank, N.A., of Pittsburgh. We are especially indebted to Adele Chatfield-Taylor, the former director of the endowment's Design Arts Program, who has encouraged the efforts of hundreds of organizations to make cities and towns more attractive, more livable and more humane.

I recommend to you the work of our authors, Richard C. Collins, Elizabeth B. Waters and A. Bruce Dotson, director, senior associate and assistant director, respectively, of the Institute for Environmental Negotiation of the University of Virginia. Besides collecting a wealth of information about preservation planning activities around the country, they have provided insightful, sensitive observations that enhance our understanding of the preservation tools and planning processes that lead to success. Their work should not only assist local government officials and preservation advocates, but also serve as a useful resource for historic preservation and urban planning study programs of universities.

Our guiding principle, as stated so well in the 1966 National Historic Preservation Act, continues to be the preservation of our nation's historic and cultural foundations "as a living part of our community life and development in order to give a sense of orientation to the American people."

J. Jackson Walter, President
National Trust for Historic Preservation

Preface

During the early 1980s, the National Trust for Historic Preservation heard many complaints about the way preservationists presented their point of view. "There is too much litigation. There are too many 11th-hour challenges to plans long since agreed to," said mayors and developers. "We want preservationists to take a more responsible role in city planning, to identify their priorities early, so everyone knows where each stands."

The frequency with which such complaints were made, coupled with a recognition that early involvement in the development of local land-use plans and zoning ordinances could significantly affect the fate of historic resources, led the National Trust to create the Critical Issues Fund (CIF) in February 1981. As stated in the original guidelines, the purpose of the program is to enable preservation advocates "to play a responsible role in the processes that will decide the future of historic properties."

During its 10 years, the CIF program has encouraged local efforts to weave preservation values into local land-use plans and zoning ordinances. These tools for guiding and shaping growth and development unleash a whole set of investment decisions, economic pressures, tax policies and political attitudes   can make it prohibitively expensive and politically difficult to protect a community's historic assets. By designating historic areas for protection, cities and towns can let developers know in advance which properties are likely to provoke a public outcry if they are slated for demolition. Given the risks that inevitably accompany the development process, it is understandable that developers value highly whatever certainty and predictability can be provided.

The first CIF grant was awarded in 1981 to the Foundation for San Francisco's Architectural Heritage (Heritage). The San Francisco planning office had turned to Heritage for information that might provide the basis for city policies for protecting local historic landmarks. "By providing reliable and complete technical information at this critical time," wrote Heritage in its grant application to the Trust, "Heritage will be able to significantly influence public opinion and the ultimate form of the city's preservation policies." The CIF-assisted study that ensued did indeed influence preservation policies in San Francisco. Most of the study's recommendations eventually found a place in the Downtown Plan approved by the city in September 1985. These included:

- Outright ban against the demolition of San Francisco's most important historic buildings;

- Transfer of development rights program, to make the retention of landmarks more economically feasible for property owners and to steer high-rise development into areas that needed new investment; and

- Establishment of six "conservation districts," each with its own height limits and design guidelines, to preserve the character of architecturally distinctive areas.

These policies remain in effect today and have played an important role in preserving much of what we all love about the City by the Bay.

Since the San Francisco project, the CIF program has supported other efforts to shape local development policies. In Atlanta, the program helped to create a new model for resolving policy conflicts between preservationists and developers. In Philadelphia, it supported a survey and analysis of major tools available for historic resource protection. In Roanoke, it backed an aggressive citizen outreach program carried out by the city as part of an effort to make a new comprehensive plan and zoning ordinance more friendly to historic preservation. And in Denver, it assisted the development of an innovative package of demolition controls, design standards, financial aid for owners of historic properties and a marketing program for the Lower Downtown Historic District.

While assisting these projects, the National Trust also became aware of important efforts taking place elsewhere to improve the quality of the urban environment. These included Boston's Interim Planning Overlay District, which reduced the allowable size and height of buildings in certain areas; Seattle's Citizens Alternative Plan, a ballot box initiative that put a lid on new downtown development as a way to protect the city's special character; and St. Paul's recycling of Lowertown, a historic warehouse district, through private foundation support, mayoral leadership and negotiated investment strategy.

America's Downtowns sifts through the information generated by these projects and identifies the most important lessons learned. What do these projects tell us about the effectiveness of various methods of protecting historic areas? About techniques for resolving preservation and development conflicts? About approaches to marshalling community resources— human as well as financial—to preserve and reuse those historic buildings and areas that citizens value greatly?

The book analyzes not only the substance of preservation policies that emerged from these local planning activities but, even more importantly, the processes and political dynamics that led to the establishment of these policies. It is often said that the easy part of creating a local preservation law is writing the ordinance; the hard part is mustering public understanding and political support for the ordinance. This is what this book is all about.

Constance Epton Beaumont

City of Paris building, San Francisco, demolished in 1981 to make way for a new department store. The structure's lobby and glass dome were incorporated in the Neiman Marcus department store erected on the site. (© 1990 Craig Buchanan)

Prospects for Historic Preservation in America's Downtowns

In spring 1989, the city of Atlanta opened a multimillion dollar retail and entertainment center in a historic area of the downtown. That same spring, Seattle voted two to one in favor of a citizens' ballot box initiative that placed an annual limit on the amount of new office space permitted downtown. To some observers, these cities might appear to have contradictory objectives: one promoting new downtown development, the other restricting it. But these actions may also reflect a common desire on the part of cities to make their downtowns more attractive, livable and economically healthy.

The 1980s saw tremendous innovation on the part of American cities to improve their downtowns, and historic preservation figured prominently in these efforts. The Downtown Master Plan approved by the San Francisco Board of Supervisors in 1985 created "conservation districts" to protect the scale and special character of the city's architecturally distinctive areas. The Downtown Area Plan, endorsed by the Denver city council in May 1986, combined demolition and urban design controls with a business promotion and marketing program to rejuvenate the Lower Downtown Historic District. That same year, Roanoke established a creative process for involving citizens in the city's new policies for balancing community conservation with new growth and development. And in 1989, the city of Atlanta created a new model for mediating historic preservation and development conflicts in the downtown.

Motivated by a desire to understand what accounts for success and failure in these and other ground-breaking downtown planning initiatives, the National Trust for Historic Preservation commissioned the Institute for Environmental Negotiation at the University of Virginia to prepare case studies of 10 major cities. In preparing the case studies that follow, institute staff tried to capture the unique stories of each city and at the same time identify common themes.

Downtown Planning and Historic Preservation

Early historic preservation efforts in this country focussed initially on the preservation of individual buildings for their historical value and architectural merit. But as early as 1961, when Jane Jacobs wrote her classic, *The Death and Life of Great American Cities*, people had begun to recognize that historic buildings and areas made an important contribution to the economic health of cities as well to their attractiveness and livability. Whether landmark theaters, libraries or museums serve as major people attractions, or whether small old buildings provide economical locations for housing or small businesses, Jacobs argued that physical preservation of cities is an important way to promote the mixture of uses and visual attractiveness that contribute to cities' economic and social success. Almost 30 years later, this is becoming a major theme in downtown plans for American cities.

Essentially all 10 cities examined here have adopted goals and strategies designed to help them increase the economic diversity of their downtowns through historic preservation. Reductions in allowable building heights in San Francisco, Seattle and Boston; design guidelines and marketing programs for historic warehouse districts in St. Paul and Denver; downtown entertainment centers in Atlanta, Roanoke and Boston; and mixed-use waterfront developments in Jersey City are all examples of attempts to increase the levels of round-the-clock activity in these cities. Quite apart from efforts to slow or encourage growth, these cities are trying to generate greater variety in downtown activities and, in many instances, historic preservation is seen as an important factor in accomplishing this. Ties between preservation and downtown housing, tourism, attractive pedestrian environments and other major downtown goals are becoming clearer.

As preservationists broaden their sights and begin to explore where preservation fits with other important downtown goals, they are taking a hard look at their role in the larger planning and decision-making process. In almost all the cities studied, attempts are under way to build links between planning for historic resource protection and planning for the broader community of which these resources are a part. We see this in Atlanta where the Department of Community Development now comments on the broader planning implications of any proposed historic designation. We see it in Denver where designation of a historic district became a central part of the city's downtown development plan. We see it in San Francisco where the downtown plan is built in large measure around the concept of preservation, and we see it in the wide range of downtown planning initiatives being undertaken in the other seven case study cities.

New Generation of Downtown Planning Initiatives

In an attempt to manage growth and encourage more urban vitality, cities are adopting new plans and revising their zoning ordinances. While all the individual cities studied have some version of a local historic preservation ordinance, many of them have added provisions for incentive zoning, transfer of development rights, interim controls and revolving loan funds to promote the kind of urban development they want, including, in many cases, the preservation of community character and historic resources.

Incentive Zoning. Since New York adopted an incentive zoning system in 1961, many cities have used this tool as a way to accommodate growth, while obtaining various public benefits. Incentive zoning allows a developer to build more space for sale or lease in a building than would otherwise be permitted. In return for being allowed to build a bigger building, the developer provides certain public benefits, such as the preservation of historic buildings, affordable housing and cultural or day care facilities. Several of the case study cities have established some kind of incentive or bonus system in an attempt to improve the quality of downtown development.

Yet many cities with bonus system experience have found that bonuses can lead to large numbers of very big buildings and shadowed streets, with few measurable public benefits. In response to these drawbacks, cities such as Seattle and Philadelphia are cutting back on the density bonuses, making certain things mandatory and incorporating more guidelines and review procedures into their bonus programs. Other cities are going even further and eliminating bonuses altogether. In Boston only a few bonus provisions remain in the city's highest density areas. San Francisco has abandoned bonuses altogether. Boston and San Francisco have also taken a further step: developers wanting to build even at "by right" heights and densities must help pay for the housing, transportation and other costs resulting from that development.

Looking at the case study cities, we can see a continuum in how cities deal with bonus zoning, which includes everything from Cincinnati with its generous new bonus system to San Francisco, which has no bonuses. Several cities fall at various stages between these two. It appears that key variables in a city's position on the bonus issue are its eagerness to promote development, citizen attitudes toward growth and the community's view concerning costs real estate development should bear.

Transfer of Development Rights. A technique related to incentive zoning, the transfer of development rights (TDR) allows the owner of a building the community wants to preserve—a historic landmark, for example—to transfer the development rights normally granted on the landmark site to another site. Thus, if the zoning permitted a 12-story building on the landmark site but the landmark is only seven stories high, the owner could transfer the difference—five stories—to a site in a zone designated to receive TDRs. If the zoning on the receiving site is too lenient, however, there may be little incentive for anyone to buy the TDRs. Also, bonus or incentive zoning may undercut the TDR program if such zoning allows for increased densities at less cost than the TDRs. TDRs have been adopted by a number of communities as one way to preserve historic structures and open spaces.

Design Review. Most cities today are using design review—and in the cases of San Francisco and Philadelphia, design requirements—as a way to encourage interesting skylines, promote attractive human-scale street level facades and minimize negative environmental impacts. Often, while this is not made explicit, the design review requirement also allows the local body empowered to grant approval or disapproval to comment on other aspects of a development proposal. From a preservation standpoint, any public review procedure is valuable because it provides a forum in which to interject preservation values into the debate.

Interim Zoning Controls. A regulatory tool downtown areas have borrowed from earlier suburban growth management efforts is interim zoning controls. This is a way of preserving the status quo while new plans and ordinances can be adopted. Boston put an Interim Planning Overlay District in place, lowering height limits citywide while new permanent zoning could be developed for individual districts. In Atlanta interim zoning protection was provided for about 152 historic structures for one year while the comprehensive preservation plan and ordinance were being finalized. To be upheld legally, interim ordinances generally should be limited to specific time periods, related to a comprehensive planning process and enacted in accordance with state laws. If established this way, they offer a useful tool for local governments to prevent last-minute efforts to gain permissions for development or demolition before new rules are adopted.

Financial Incentives. In addition to regulatory measures designed to promote more livable downtowns, cities are employing a wide range of financial incentives as well. Many of these focus specifically on encouraging preservation. The cities of Denver, Roanoke and St. Paul have established revolving loan funds to help owners of historic buildings finance rehabilitation. In the case of Denver, the fund was part of a package to get the new downtown district designated as historic. In the cases of Roanoke and St. Paul, the fund resulted from strong public-private partnerships formed as part of overall urban revitalization efforts. Both Atlanta and Philadelphia are working on financial incentives for preservation that include substantial tax abatements. Other innovative financial incentives being offered by various cities include Atlanta's housing enterprise zones, which extend tax benefits to both new and rehabilitated housing within these zones, and direct investment of foundation funds to promote reha- bilitation of historic structures through St. Paul's Lowertown Redevelop- ment Corporation. It can be argued that it makes good economic as well as good preservation sense not merely to protect buildings from demolition, but also to see that these buildings become contributing elements in the city's economy.

Plan Development and Implementation

Downtown planning is becoming a negotiated process, integrally re- lated to plan implementation, although cities vary in their ability to imple- ment plans once they are developed. The plan development phase involves establishing basic community goals. At this stage it is relatively easy for a community to embrace a broad set of goals that can include everything from economic development to affordable housing to historic preservation without having to face some of the difficult choices that emerge in the execution of these goals. The implementation phase of downtown planning is the point at which zoning must be changed, public dollars invested and other actions taken to transform a plan into reality. This involves setting priorities and making trade-offs. For preservation to be fully integrated into downtown decision making, preservation values must be strongly articulated during both the development and implementation phases.

The challenge involved in sustaining preservation interests through the implementation phase can be seen in several case study cities. In Denver, even after the downtown plan was adopted, a major challenge still lay ahead to get the Lower Downtown Historic District ordinance passed. The ordinance included, among other things, strong anti-demolition con- trols for this district. Getting the city council to adopt the ordinance required building coalitions with other downtown interests, providing a revolving loan fund and accepting a biennial review of the ordinance's effects on the economic health of Lower Downtown. While the overall package fell short of what some preservationists had hoped for, getting a new historic district in the heart of downtown is something few cities have managed to do in recent years and it was a significant accomplishment. Cincinnati preservationists succeeded in including the concept of a down- town historic district in their new downtown plan, but they found little support when they moved to the plan implementation phase.

Coalition Building

Looking across cities, no single "right" way to influence the downtown decision-making process emerges. As many kinds of institutional arrange- ments exist as there are cities. Some have suggested that understanding a city's style of doing business will help determine what kind of approach to use: grass-roots, high-level negotiation or other processes. While in each city the coalitions formed are different, some similarities can be identified.

Cities have many entities, public and private, which must cooperate for downtown planning and development to take place. In most cities, however, there is one office or entity within the governmental structure that plays the central role in downtown development. In San Francisco, the city's planning commission has extraordinary powers to implement the comprehensive plan. In Boston, the Boston Redevelopment Authority enjoys the combined power of a planning commission and a redevelopment authority. In Jersey City, the Department of Housing and Economic Development fosters downtown growth. In St. Paul, several key participants play a role, including the mayor's office, the Lowertown Redevelopment Corporation and the port authority. The powers wielded by major players in buying and selling land, controlling development rights and in other ways intervening in the development process make them important partners to anyone interested in shaping the future of downtowns.

While preservation advocates are working hard to align themselves with powerful forces within the governmental structure, they also have begun to build coalitions with other interest groups. Alliances preservationists have formed with business interests to build lively downtowns are playing an important role in Atlanta and Denver. Neighborhood activists have been strong allies of preservation in Roanoke, Jersey City and elsewhere, and these partnerships have the potential to grow stronger as issues of neighborhood revitalization, downtown housing and affordable housing become more important. Preservationists in Boston and San Francisco have succeeded in joining forces with urban open-space advocates who are concerned about buildings blocking light and shading existing parks. Both groups tend to favor lower height limits and stronger requirements for community open space.

Preservationists share common ground with urban designers in their commitment to good civic design and to relationships between buildings and streetscapes that enhance social activities. Both are interested in urban fabric, the beauty of individual buildings and their relationship to one another. In some instances, however, their interests do not entirely overlap. In the same way that preservationists find themselves at odds with neighborhood and housing organizations over the gentrification issue, they find themselves in conflict with urban design enthusiasts when the issue involves using transfer of development rights to allow bigger, taller buildings on certain sites in order to preserve historic buildings on others. This may seem a rational trade if your goal is to save individual landmarks, but for those who are most interested in the relationships between buildings and the general scale of development, allowing overdevelopment on one site in favor of another may seem a blinkered, short-sighted policy. The chief lesson here is that coalitions must be formed and realigned constantly in the ever-changing landscape of urban politics.

In addition to the coalitions that can be formed between interest groups, relationships between preservation review bodies, planning commissions and the staffs of those entities have a major effect on the success of preservation agendas. Cities are responding to the increased scope of historic preservation decisions by making local review bodies more representative of affected interests, not just those with special expertise in historic preservation. As part of its new preservation program, the city of Atlanta altered the membership of its Urban Design Commission to include people with real estate and development expertise to allow a fuller debate on issues involved in protecting historic buildings and districts. Philadelphia has an unusual arrangement whereby the major city department heads and the president of the city council sit on the preservation review panel along with architectural historians and real estate developers. Strong preservationists might argue such a group is not in as good a position to evaluate historical significance as one that includes stronger representation of architects and historians. On the other hand, such a panel potentially allows better integration of preservation considerations with all other downtown planning decisions. In general, the more a review panel represents broad community interests, the greater amount of power it is given for key decisions. The less representative it is, the more vulnerable its actions seem to mayoral vetoes and appeals to city councils.

Like all interest groups, preservationists must deal with tensions within the preservation community. A shortage of staffing and resources for local landmarks commissions sometimes creates tension between these organizations and advocacy groups. Advocacy groups often think commissions are not aggressive enough in pursuing additional historic building designations or stringent enough in their reviews of proposed development projects. The commissions, on the other hand, worry about taking on more than they can handle and about the necessity of balancing preservation interests with other community concerns. Coalition building and alliances within city government and within the preservation community will be key variables for preservation advocates, just as they are for any group trying to influence the public decision-making process.

Collaborative Planning and Negotiation

As public policy choices are becoming more difficult and complex, people responsible for public decision making are looking for new approaches to set priorities and resolve conflicts. The environmental and preservation laws of the 1960s gave citizen activists many avenues to challenge public decisions but they did not necessarily provide forums for improved decision making. The case studies show that city governments are among those looking for innovative processes as a way to build some consensus around critical issues. These processes usually involve bringing together individuals representing the broad spectrum of interests that surround any issue. Such forums tend to have an equalizing effect among the voices around a table and in that sense provide preservationists and other traditionally weaker players an unusual opportunity to present their cases and try to develop common ground with more powerful groups.

Several of the case study cities illustrate the use of innovative collaborative planning processes. In two of the cities, lengthy structured negotiation processes were used, in Denver to develop a new downtown plan and in Atlanta to develop a comprehensive preservation program. In both Denver and Atlanta, outside mediator-facilitators were used to convene the various interests and help focus the negotiations. Boston's new zoning for the Midtown Cultural District was developed in a similar manner, with negotiations among all interested parties mediated by staff from the Boston Redevelopment Authority. In 1985 Roanoke launched an extensive grassroots collaborative planning process, which included community meetings, workshops and call-in television shows. Preservationists worked side by side with neighborhood activists and downtown enthusiasts throughout the process, and the plan and ordinance that emerged carried a strong preservation orientation.

Preservation advocates involved in these collaborative planning processes caution others about the time, energy and perseverance it takes to participate in such endeavors. They have been able to use these new forums to achieve significant successes and to alter their community's view of preservation. Most people acknowledge, however, that this kind of participation, often by volunteers, is extremely demanding. If, as it appears, collaborative planning is a path more communities intend to follow, the preservation community and others will have to explore ways to provide better preparation and support for the representatives they send to the bargaining table.

Looking to the Future

The preservation movement at present appears strong and broad enough to encompass many different priorities and interests. The relationships between historic preservation, urban planning and downtown development are changing, with important political implications. In a sense, historic preservation has become less a separate movement and more a philosophy of urban planning and design. With preservation advocates joining those concerned about the environmental and social qualities of cities and their downtowns, the entire landscape of downtown planning and decision making is changing.

As preservation moves beyond concern for protecting individual buildings to issues of preserving community character, scale and fabric, it is entering some of the most challenging and provocative territory in urban planning today. As those concerned with community preservation no longer focus just on designating landmarks and historic districts but pursue concepts like conservation districts, they are bringing larger and more varied areas under the protection umbrella. As they try to define what is meant by community character and set guidelines review boards can use to determine whether certain changes are or are not in keeping with this character, they will find themselves pushing the limits of what is permitted in the way of zoning for aesthetic purposes. Different rules and standards are being set for different kinds of districts and the lines are becoming increasingly blurred between preservation, neighborhood planning and growth management. As this happens, preservationists and others will be testing the law to see how far local government can go to control the shape and rate of change in our communities in the future.

Looking ahead, preservationists and others would do well to note the strength of public sentiment being expressed through elections, citizen initiatives and referenda about a wide range of quality-of-life issues. It suggests that in some localities, at least, the pace or direction of official action is lagging behind what the citizenry wants. A growing constituency is demanding action to protect communities and factors that contribute to their livability. The time is ripe for a new era in leadership, planning and consensus building to make America's cities what their inhabitants want them to be. The case studies offered in this book suggest preservationists have a significant role in this, if they want to and are willing to expand their vision, concerns and efforts to make it happen.

Flatiron Building, Atlanta's oldest surviving skyscraper, located in the Fairlie-Poplar District, an area under study for permanent protection under Atlanta's recently strengthened preservation ordinance. (Atlanta Urban Design Commission)

Atlanta

Preservation politics in Atlanta, Ga., heated up in spring 1986. An *Atlanta Constitution* editorial sounded this warning:

> Some 300 apartment units were demolished last December (for reasons that remain murky) . . . . If the 74 units of the Peachtree Terrace go, the neighborhood will have lost some 400 to 500 residences . . . . Soon the small eateries and other folksy amenities nearby will be left with only an office hours clientele, and Pershing Point (where Peachtree Terrace is located) will become much like downtown: an after-hours ghost town . . . . City Hall should deny the Peachtree Terrace demolition permit.

The city council did deny the demolition permit, but its decision was vetoed by Mayor Andrew Young. The newspapers were filled with letters to the editor, charges and countercharges. While the city council tried unsuccessfully to get a series of new preservation ordinances adopted, historic buildings continued to be demolished, leaving parking lots in their wake.

Against this background, a mediated negotiation process was set up that included the mayor, several members of the city council and other leaders in the business, development and preservation communities. The purpose of the negotiations was to try to put an end to the warfare and to seek agreement on a historic preservation program that would be consistent with the city's broader development goals. In June 1988, after 10 months of intense negotiation, all parties did reach agreement. A year later, Atlanta's new historic preservation ordinance was adopted by a 19 to 0 vote of the full city council.

The City

Atlanta's story is one of a young city on the move, hurrying to catch up. Founded in 1847, the city is less than 150 years old. General Sherman's siege and burning of Atlanta in 1864 destroyed most of the city, but five years after the war, Atlanta was almost completely rebuilt and its population had doubled.

The latter part of the 19th century was an era of rapid development, centered around Atlanta's rail lines and depot. The city promoted itself by holding several international expositions. In 1891 the Equitable Building, Atlanta's first skyscraper, was constructed. Thus began the process that would transform the skyline of central Atlanta through the first half of the 20th century from low transport-oriented warehouses to high-rise office buildings and hotels.

Since the 1960s metropolitan Atlanta has been a major regional center in the Southeast. It has the busiest airport in the country and is home to countless government and private sector regional offices. During the 1970s, corporate interest in the burgeoning suburbs around Atlanta ushered in a period of economic stagnation for the center city. Total population declined, the portion of the population living in poverty increased, and crime rates soared.

When elected in 1981, Mayor Andrew Young was determined to launch what he called the "second rebirth" of the city of Atlanta. He made economic revitalization of the city the centerpiece of his administration and, judging by some of the more traditional economic indicators, Young's strategy of investment and promotion has had a positive effect. Atlanta added about 30 million square feet of new office space from 1983 to 1987—almost doubling downtown office space, from 44 million square feet in 1983 to more than 70 million in 1987. As in many cities, this development was accompanied by a significant increase in the office vacancy rate, which now hovers around 20 percent. Office construction, however, has not slowed significantly.

Atlanta is a major center of African-American culture in this country. Atlanta University's five colleges, whose foundations reach back to Reconstruction, have produced generations of prominent black leaders. The area known as Sweet Auburn, a street of two- and three-story small shops and residences immediately adjacent to the gleaming new towers of downtown Atlanta, was the cradle of black entrepreneurship in this country following the Civil War. Atlanta also played a central role in the Civil Rights Movement of the 1960s. In 1987 the city designated the Martin Luther King/Sweet Auburn District as a Historic Conservation District, recognizing two of the most important eras in African-American history in this city.

Atlanta is the home base of architect and developer John Portman, popularizer of the multistory atrium lobby. Portman's vision for Atlanta has been to create attractive enclosed environments built around convention hotel facilities. To make his vision a reality, Portman founded a development company that acquired large blocks of downtown real estate under the city's urban renewal program. He launched an era of self-contained megastructures with meeting rooms, restaurants and shops that people come to, stay in and leave without ever venturing out into the city. Reproduced in cities across the country, these self-contained environments, such as pedestrian skywalks, have been criticized by many for pulling activity and vitality off city streets. This is one of many issues current downtown planning in Atlanta is trying to address.

Planning Framework

Development in Atlanta is guided by a series of plans that have been adopted by the city, with substantial input from the business community. In 1973, prompted by the building of the MARTA rapid transit system, Atlanta adopted a citywide development plan entitled the Atlanta Urban Framework Plan. The major purpose of this plan was to identify how the rapid transit system should be used as a catalyst to stimulate future growth and development. The city settled on a node and spine plan that called for development concentrated along major corridors, around transit stations and within a Central Business District. While political administrations have come and gone during the 16 years since this plan was adopted, it has remained the blueprint for development. The highest density zoning continues to exist in these corridors and nodes.

The effect of this overall plan can be seen in the Midtown section of the city, about 20 city blocks north of downtown along the Peachtree Street corridor. The 1973 plan and zoning ordinance created Special Public Interest Districts around the three Midtown MARTA stations. In these districts the city allowed the tallest buildings found anywhere outside the Central Business District. The result has been the addition of the IBM Tower, the Georgia Pacific headquarters building, Trammel Crow's 999 Peachtree Street and many other multistory showcase buildings. These have replaced the low-rise buildings that lined Peachtree Street and housed people, shops, restaurants and a variety of arts activities.

In addition to the Atlanta Urban Framework Plan, the city has a comprehensive development plan that is updated every year. The plan includes separate chapters dealing with economic development, transportation, human services, environmental protection, urban design and preservation, among other issues. The chapter on comprehensive development recommends specific actions to be taken, while the urban design and preservation chapter outlines projects that are part of the year's agenda including district guidelines to be developed and specific streetscape projects to be undertaken.

The private business community has taken the primary lead in planning for Atlanta's downtown area. Atlanta is home to one of the strongest downtown business organizations in the country. Central Atlanta Progress (C.A.P.), founded by major downtown property owners, is a business and civic association formed to put together cooperative projects between business and local government. In 1971 C.A.P. completed a Central Area Study for the city that called for a series of initiatives to spur development. With that plan largely complete, in the mid-1980s C.A.P. turned its energies to a new Central Area Study, CAS II, to focus on improvements in many areas, including housing, arts and entertainment, infrastructure, public safety and urban design. CAS II, developed jointly by the city and C.A.P., represents another chapter in the alliance between business and government that has characterized Atlanta politics and planning for most of its recent history.

During the early part of the 1980s, visions of a rebuilt city of gleaming office towers left little room for the preservation of historic buildings. These buildings often were seen as an impediment to the city's economic success. In the last year or two a subtle shift has occurred. The desire to stabilize and increase the amount of in-town housing has focused greater attention on Atlanta's neighborhoods and old apartment structures. Both the mayor's office and C.A.P. have become concerned about Atlanta's image as a 9-to-5 city that visitors leave as soon as business is done. Trying to change this is what lies behind CAS II, which emphasizes urban design, livability and creating a more vital 24-hour city. This changing climate helped set the stage for the new preservation planning initiative.

New Preservation Initiative

Until recently, historic preservation in Atlanta consisted of strict rules for a few selected districts and weak protection for a larger collection of historic sites and districts. No significant protection was provided for individual landmark buildings, and a large number of buildings and districts eligible for the National Register of Historic Places had no protection at all.

As already mentioned, by summer 1986 tensions were mounting over the loss of a number of turn-of-the-century apartment buildings along Peachtree Street. Despite his known interest in increasing in-town housing opportunities, Mayor Young seemed unsympathetic to preservation concerns. People in city government and elsewhere who knew about the use of mediated negotiations decided to try this process to build consensus for historic preservation in Atlanta.

With support from city government, C.A.P., the Atlanta Preservation Center, a $33,450 Critical Issues Fund grant from the National Trust for Historic Preservation and a supplemental grant from the National Institute for Dispute Resolution, the city hired a team of mediators from the Southeast Negotiation Network at the Georgia Institute of Technology and the Institute for Environmental Negotiation at the University of Virginia to convene and facilitate a historic preservation steering committee. The committee, composed of key individuals from city government, business leaders and preservation advocates, was charged with developing a comprehensive historic preservation program for the city.

From the beginning, the process received strong support from the mayor's office, apparently because of a sense that the ongoing conflict was costly in time, energy and resources. Mayor Young signed the letter of application for the National Trust grant. He and key members of his staff agreed to serve on the steering committee, and he extended the letter of invitation to other committee members requesting that they serve.

Fundamental issues facing the committee were: does a city that burned to the ground in 1864 have anything worth saving, and if so, what does it look like, and what is its value? A subset of this issue was presented by the debate over the preservation of the architecturally unremarkable but historic house in which Margaret Mitchell wrote *Gone with the Wind*: why would city leadership want to preserve elements of a period of history many of its citizens want to forget? Another major question was what, if any, place is there for preservation values in a city that is emphasizing economic development, and trying to attract large amounts of new investment and build its tax base? Why put constraints on property and owners and what kinds of offsetting incentives might make this more palatable? These and other issues were addressed during the negotiation process. In the end, the success of this process depended not on convincing everyone that historic buildings should be saved for their own sake, but on linking the goals of preservation to broader, more widely held goals related to building a vital downtown.

Negotiation Process

The negotiation process itself consisted of monthly sessions--usually lasting three to four hours--over a 10-month period. The financial support available through the Critical Issues Fund grant allowed the team of mediators to recruit national legal, economic and preservation experts to discuss private property rights, reasonable economic return, interim development controls, historical significance and other sensitive issues ultimately at the heart of designing a preservation program. Background papers were prepared and distributed on these topics. (These are available from the National Trust for Historic Preservation as part of its Critical Issues Series and titles appear at the end of this case study.)

Among those brought in to meet with the committee members were Robert H. Freilich, a nationally known land-use expert, and Richard J. Roddewig, an expert in preservation law and economics, who addressed a range of legal and economic issues. Frederick C. Williamson, Sr., state historic preservation officer for Rhode Island, and former director of the Rhode Island Department of Community Affairs, offered perspectives on the value of historic preservation to the community as a whole. In addition, local preservation experts from the state historic preservation office, the

Georgia Trust for Historic Preservation, and the city's Urban Design Commission provided technical assistance throughout the process. This diverse group of experts provided a broad base of knowledge to committee members and helped to reduce competition and friction about who would take credit for this effort and any successes.

Early meetings were largely educational so that all participants could reach a common level of understanding with respect to basic historic preservation, zoning and real estate development concepts. With such an understanding established, it was assumed that the group would have an easier time reaching agreement on specific provisions proposed for the preservation program. Although this assumption proved valid, an agreement still did not come easily.

Proposals to limit what owners of historic buildings could do with their property were seen by some committee members as an infringement on private property rights. A proposal to provide interim protection for buildings nominated to be, but not yet officially designated as, historic landmarks was initially strongly resisted by the development community while preservationists considered such protection critical lest important buildings be lost while the negotiations continued.

A major concern of developers and city officials alike was that restrictions on landmarks would cause Atlanta to lose businesses to the adjacent suburbs, where no similar restrictions applied, thus eroding the city's tax base. Aided by research conducted by the Georgia Trust for Historic Preservation, the preservation community was able to demonstrate that a large percentage of Atlanta's historic landmarks had been demolished in recent years, not for new development that helped the city's tax base, but rather for surface parking lots that blighted the city and made it less attractive to new investment.

During the final stages of the negotiation process, task forces were formed to take up major topics. These included economic incentives for preservation, the historic designation process and levels of protection to be provided for different resources. Finally, following nine months of arduous negotiations, the committee reached agreement on a comprehensive historic preservation program for the city of Atlanta.

Agreement Reached

The comprehensive preservation program negotiated by the steering committee (and eventually adopted by the city council in an extensive amendment to the zoning ordinance) greatly strengthened the protection given to historic resources in Atlanta.

The new preservation ordinance provides for five different levels of protection for buildings and districts:
  1.Landmark Buildings and Sites
  2.Landmark Districts

Former Atlanta Mayor Andrew Young, applauded by city council members and others after signing the comprehensive historic preservation plan recommendations agreed to by the Historic Preservation Steering Committee with the help of mediators. (Marvin Hill, Jr., Atlanta Journal and Constitution)

The strongest protection is provided for Landmark Buildings and contributing buildings in Landmark Districts. For these buildings, demolition or alteration is allowed only if a threat to public health or safety is present or if preservation is economically infeasible, and only if the property owner can submit evidence of plans and financial ability to construct a replacement building. Even when all conditions are met, the city has 60 days to prepare a preservation plan and solicit public or private buyers to prevent a landmark's demolition.

3.Historic Buildings and Sites

4.Historic Districts

Historic Buildings and contributing buildings in Historic Districts enjoy a reduced level of protection. They can be demolished only if the owner already has detailed plans and financing in place for a replacement building and has received a foundation permit from the city to begin work on the new structure.

5.Conservation Districts

In Conservation Districts only advisory comment is possible on any plans to alter or demolish buildings in those districts.

A particularly strong feature of the Atlanta law is that Landmark District designation can replace existing zoning provisions for a district, thus changing previously applicable height and land-use requirements. That allows the city to establish height and density allowances and specific-use restrictions suited to the character of a district as part of the historic designation process, along with the more traditional restrictions on alteration and demolition. The result is that within these districts, the classic tension that often exists between protection for historic structures and underlying zoning is generally eliminated.

Throughout the negotiation process, providing financial assistance to owners of designated landmarks was seen as crucial, and the final agreement called for a number of economic incentives: tax abatements, freezes on the tax assessments on renovated historic buildings at their pre-rehabilitation value, a revolving loan fund, an endangered buildings program designed to identify and intervene economically in the fate of threatened buildings, and a preservation marketing program. No action has been taken yet on the revolving loan fund, the endangered buildings program or the marketing program. The city did extend the tax benefits available in its housing enterprise zones to include rehabilitated housing as well as new construction.

Of all the financial incentives proposed in the agreement, the development community felt most strongly about the ones that would provide tax freezes for Landmark Buildings. As the zoning package was being developed and negotiated, developers were adamant that the incentives had to be included to guarantee their support. There were two major hurdles. Under current Georgia law, tax freezes are not generally permitted. In addition, the city council's finance staff had not been able to complete an analysis of the cost of this provision to the city. A final compromise was struck whereby the law would be adopted without the incentives, the city would go to the state for the necessary enabling legislation to allow tax abatement, and the financial analysis would be completed. The law contained a sunset clause stating that, if for any reason the city did not adopt the incentive package within one year of the adoption of the original law, then all buildings designated as landmarks would be automatically reclassified as Historic Buildings, thus reducing their level of protection.

Administration of the New Ordinance

The provisions of the zoning code dealing with historic preservation are administered by an 11-member Urban Design Commission appointed by the mayor. As part of the negotiated agreement, commission membership was reduced from 16 to 11 and requirements for one member each from the real estate, land development and legal professions were added to existing requirements that the commission include architects, artists and preservationists. The intent in reducing the size and altering the composition of the commission was to improve its ability to function efficiently and make balanced decisions that take historic, aesthetic, legal and economic aspects into account.

The Urban Design Commission is responsible for nominating structures and districts for protection. As part of the designation process, the new law provides that, in addition to the standard documentation provided by the commission, the Bureau of Planning will prepare a report outlining larger community development considerations as they relate to a proposed designation, including but not limited to a description of the building or area, the existing zoning classification, the need for transitional zones to serve as buffers, and the economic incentives available including the transfer of development rights. This was seen as an important way to be sure that preservation planning and decision making were seen as integral parts of broader planning and development decisions.

Once a historic building or district nomination is prepared, the planning bureau's report completed and public hearings held, the final historic designation decisions are made by the city council. Once a property is designated, final decisions regarding requests to alter or demolish the structure are made by the Urban Design Commission with appeal only to the Superior Court. This feature of the Atlanta ordinance removes an avenue of political appeal left open elsewhere, as many other cities permit city councils to overturn such decisions.

Special Features

There are two special features contained in Atlanta's new legislation that deserve additional comment: an economic review panel to determine reasonable economic return and interim controls.

Economic Review Panel. Permission to demolish any landmark or any contributing building in a landmark district requires the owner to demonstrate that a reasonable economic return cannot be achieved using carefully itemized criteria. This documentation is given to a three-person Economic Review Panel consisting of three real estate and redevelopment professionals, one panel member selected by the Urban Design Commission, one by the applicant and one by the first two appointees. The panel then makes a determination as to whether or not an economic hardship exists. Its decision is advisory to the Urban Design Commission but can only be overruled by a three-fourths majority of the commission and only on the basis that the Economic Review Panel "acted in an arbitrary manner, or that [its] report was based on an erroneous finding of a material fact." This process for making economic hardship decisions was developed during the negotiation process and seemed to meet the concern on all sides that the process be as fair and objective as possible.

Interim Controls. Given the rate at which historic buildings were being lost in Atlanta, providing some interim protection for historic buildings during the negotiation process was a major concern to preservationists. They tried to establish interim protection for all National Register-eligible structures at the start of the negotiations but failed.

In remarks delivered to the steering committee at one of its initial meetings, land-use attorney Robert H. Freilich stated:

> In order to protect districts or structures during the period when an ordinance is being prepared, it is valuable to provide in the enabling legislation for a period preceding adoption of the ordinance or amendments during which no alterations or demolitions can occur to specific structures or to any structure within a district. Interim controls serve a number of purposes:
>
> 1.Interim controls provide a framework or structure for the planning process and represent timetables for an extremely complex process;
>
> 2.They protect the planning or plan amendment process during its formulation and development insuring that planning itself does take place;
>
> 3.They prevent new nonconforming uses or, in the instance of historic preservation, prevent the destruction or alteration of important historic structures; and
>
> 4.They promote public debate on issues, goals and policies of the plan or amendment and development techniques proposed to implement the plan.

Freilich indicated to the committee that Georgia law allowed ample authority to implement such controls, but at this point business and development community representatives were reluctant to consider such a proposal. (This paper is cited at the end of the case study.)

Once the group reached agreement on a first round of buildings proposed for nomination and designation under the new program, the issue of interim controls was raised again. What would keep these buildings, which everyone on the steering committee had agreed should be preserved, from being demolished during the time it took the city council to adopt the ordinance and consider the nominations?

The mayor had serious reservations about the political, legal and economic implications of interim controls. He was already aware of development plans that might affect some of the buildings proposed for interim protection. In the end, the mayor was convinced there was merit in providing the time necessary for the political process to work. When he signed the agreement outlining the comprehensive program, he simultaneously signed an executive order providing 45 days of interim protection for 152 historic buildings and two districts listed in the agreement. The city council took the matter up immediately and extended the interim protection for a full year to allow time to adopt the ordinance and consider the properties for designation.

In Atlanta's pro-development climate, these interim controls were a major preservation victory and cause for considerable celebration within the preservation community. As part of the ordinance eventually adopted, the city also provided 120 days of interim protection for buildings nominated for landmark or historic designation.

Conclusion

The success of the historic preservation negotiations in Atlanta rested upon a number of factors. The support and participation of the mayor and four members of the Atlanta city council were key to the ultimate acceptance of elements contained in the agreement. The participation of top management from Portman Properties and Trammell Crow, two of the major developers in the city, meant that hard economic and legal questions were asked and answered and it gave the process credibility in the business and development communities.

Another factor that contributed to the effort's success was that the time was right for preservationists to begin new coalition building. Neighborhood protection advocates were already sympathetic to the preservationist viewpoint. During the negotiation process preservationists were able to develop common ground with Central Atlanta Progress, which, in developing the Central Area Study II, had determined that urban design, pedestrian amenities and round-the-clock activities were key to downtown vitality. C.A.P. was trying to keep people in the city and on its streets and saw a variety of historic buildings and areas as important in accomplishing that goal. Major investment made by C.A.P. and the city in a centrally located retail and entertainment district called Underground Atlanta (itself at one time a National Register historic district before extensive fire damage) contributed to this meeting of the minds. New alliances were developed between the preservation community and those concerned with black heritage and history. The common interests that existed between downtown housing advocates and those who wanted to save historic apartment houses were crystallized. In the end, it was a combination of mutual education and converging agendas that allowed for an agreement.

Atlanta is and will remain for the foreseeable future a major growth center in the Southeast. The new respect given to the protection of historic resources is a result not of a desire to slow or limit growth, but a desire to capture the contribution preservation can make to advancing Atlanta into the ranks of international caliber cities. We are not likely to see caps or quotas on development of the sort established in recent years in San Francisco and Seattle. What we do see is a new awareness of the role historic preservation and good urban design can play in Atlanta's efforts to create a vital 24-hour-a-day environment downtown.

At this point it is impossible to evaluate the ultimate effectiveness of this program. The city's Urban Design Commission and a number of volunteer consultants worked feverishly to get the first round of nominations completed for city council consideration while they were still under interim protection. To date, the city council has designated 34 buildings as landmarks and eight as historic sites. The council has denied landmark designation to only four buildings, but it did hand preservationists a major disappointment in refusing to designate the 10-block area downtown, Fairlie Poplar District, a Landmark District. Instead the council ordered a 12-month study to devise ways to revive the district's economic health while preserving its historic fabric. Interim protection has been provided for the buildings pending the outcome of the study, however.

In the meantime, the Georgia legislature has approved state enabling legislation permitting the city to provide tax freezes for income-producing landmark buildings, as called for in the original package, and the city council approved such a freeze in June 1990. Assuming the program survives, the reach of preservation protection has been broadened significantly and many more city government and business leaders understand the role preservation can play in achieving other downtown revitalization goals.

References

Atlanta Comprehensive Historic Preservation Program. Historic Preservation Policy Committee, August 8, 1988.

Central Area Study II. City of Atlanta, Central Atlanta Progress, Fulton County, February 17, 1988.

"City of Atlanta Adopts Comprehensive Historic Preservation Ordinance." Robert A. Zoeckler, *Preservation Law Reporter*, volume 8, 1989.

"Economic Incentives for Historic Preservation." Richard J. Roddewig. Critical Issues Series Report, National Trust for Historic Preservation, 1988.

"Fiscal Incentives for Historic Preservation." Susan Robinson and John E. Petersen. Critical Issues Series Report, National Trust for Historic Preservation, 1989.

"Growth Management and Historic Preservation." Robert H. Freilich and Terri A. Muren. Critical Issues Series Report, National Trust for Historic Preservation, March 1988.

Boston's Quincy Market. (David Cubbage)

Boston

In November 1984 Robert Campbell wrote in the *Boston Globe*:

> Boston may very well be looking at a beautiful future, one in which it leads the rest of America into a new era of the healthy, clean, livable, prosperous post-industrial city. Or it may be facing the disaster of chaotic and thoughtless over-building.
>
> We can make the mistake of forgetting our past and shaping our future in the image of the giant, sprawling City of Cars and Towers, an image that has hypnotized much of the world. Or we can instead learn from our past how to shape a new and better image of what all cities can become in the future. . . . We're at a moment of choice, the first such moment since a generation ago, because we've just finished executing one plan and we don't have a new one.

Three years later Boston, Mass., Mayor Raymond L. Flynn unveiled a new downtown plan for the city. The plan proposed significant height restrictions on new downtown development in an attempt to channel growth and preserve the city's character and fabric. It recommended interim zoning protection for the entire downtown area while more permanent zoning could be developed. It called for stronger design review procedures for new construction, limited development bonuses for such things as day-care space and rehabilitation of historic buildings and an ambitious program to extend the benefits of the downtown office boom out into the city's neighborhoods.

Most of Mayor Flynn's plan was translated into law, giving Boston one of the most ambitious downtown growth management programs in the country. A recent cooling off in the local economy makes it difficult to evaluate the full impact of this plan, but few doubt it will have a major effect on the city's skyline in the coming decade.

Preservationists consider the height limits and other aspects of the growth management program particularly crucial to historic resource protection in downtown Boston. In an unusual feature, state enabling legislation requires a two-thirds vote of the Boston city council to designate historic districts in the downtown area. The recent attempts to get interim protection for potential landmarks in the downtown area, which had been proposed in the mayor's plan, have failed. While there are 27 designated landmarks in downtown Boston and a number of other buildings protected by historic easements, a large number of downtown historic buildings have no direct protection from demolition or alteration. As a result, Boston will be a major test case for how far height and density limits and design review requirements will go in saving historic buildings that lack any landmark or historic district protection.

The City

The settlement of Boston dates back to 1630 when John Winthrop brought the Massachusetts Bay Colony to New England. Boston began as a trading town and served as this country's major port of entry. The young city flourished and by 1720 it was the largest town in America, with 12,000 people.

During the next century, Boston began its transformation from a trade economy to a manufacturing economy. Such notable buildings as the Old State House, North Church, Faneuil Hall and Quincy Market were added to the landscape. In 1866 the filling of Back Bay was completed, adding 100 acres of land for new development in the city.

In the 1890s Boston's economy faltered. Traditional manufacturing activities began to move out of the area and relatively little new building took place. Several decades later urbanologist Lewis Mumford said Boston should be grateful for this economic slowdown:

> That stagnation left you with fewer new buildings, with fewer new economic enterprises in the heart of Boston than were created in other cities like New York and Chicago and Minneapolis. If Boston avoided some of the economic prosperity of the years following the '90's, it also avoided some of the mistakes.

As Mumford spoke in 1957, Boston had only two genuinely tall buildings, the Custom House Tower and the John Hancock Building. Mumford urged the city leadership in its struggle against a new round of economic doldrums not to seek to match the skylines of New York but to hold onto Boston's past. It was advice city leaders chose not to follow.

In 1960 the city launched a major urban renewal program. Ed Logue, who had masterminded the renewal of New Haven, Conn., was brought in to head the Boston Redevelopment Authority (BRA), the city's urban renewal agency. The powers of the BRA were greatly enhanced by eliminating the city's planning commission and transferring its powers to the

BRA, thus giving the latter responsibility for plan development and project review along with the traditional urban renewal powers to float bonds, take land by eminent domain and sell or lease it to private developers. The BRA used these broad powers to initiate major renewal projects including the multiblock Government Center and the Prudential Center. During this same period the city abolished a citywide height limit that had been in place since 1924 restricting new buildings to 155 feet. The skyline began to change dramatically. Hundreds of historic buildings and major portions of neighborhoods were destroyed. Some argued it was urban renewal of the worst kind. Others saw it as the city's economic salvation.

One major legacy of that era is the unique combination of powers vested in the Boston Redevelopment Authority today. In addition to its planning, zoning and land acquisition activities, the BRA maintains a large research division whose economic forecasts on future space demands are credited with guiding the introduction of major projects by the private sector and with setting the pace for the BRA's development review process. During the height of the city's urban renewal program, many people objected to the almost unlimited power of the BRA. This power continues to concern some people, because of the lack of formal checks and balances on the BRA and its decision-making processes. Others argue that the city's vocal citizenry serves as an adequate check on any potential abuse of power and that the centralized power of the BRA is what allows the city to get things done.

By the early 1980s, through the efforts of the BRA and others, Boston had added 20 million square feet of new office space and had the lowest vacancy rate in the country. Fear of economic stagnation was a dim memory, replaced for many by fear of too much development. There was concern that the city's character was being eroded by all the new large-scale office development. In the same article cited in the opening paragraph of this case study, *Boston Globe* architectural critic Robert Campbell wrote:

> The old plan came out of the late 1950s and '60s, a time when, because Boston seemed to be dying, Bostonians got together and created a remarkable plan to revive the city. . . . But it's time to realize that the old plan is exhausted. . . . We go on building in an unplanned proliferation that now threatens to choke us with our own success. We still need to grow, but our growth needs to be channeled so it won't run amok. And the outlying neighborhoods need to share in the bounty.

Campbell was not alone in his thinking. Boston was on the verge of a new era in downtown development planning.

Mayor Flynn's Plan to Manage Growth

In 1983 Boston elected Mayor Raymond Flynn, a populist who grew up in the blue collar Irish Catholic neighborhood of South Boston. Mayor Flynn's campaign message was that while the new downtown office space was generating thousands of new jobs, Boston's share of the "Massachusetts Miracle" was going to wealthy corporations and suburban workers, while its citizens and neighborhoods were being left farther and farther behind. Once elected, he charged his top staff, including Stephen Coyle, director of the Boston Redevelopment Authority, with developing a plan to get a handle on downtown office development, preserve the character of the city, and extend the benefits of the boom to the city's neighborhoods.

What emerged finally in May 1987 was a dramatic proposal for encouraging economic development in a context of neighborood preservation and revitalization and growth management. In presenting A Plan to Manage Growth, Mayor Flynn said:

> Our strategy must address the twin aspects of true historic preservation: One, the protection of individual landmarks. And two, the protection of the scale, design, and architectural essence that make up the uniqueness of Boston's core cityscape. . . . Our generation has the task of finally bringing together the economic forces of the new Boston with the spirit of historic Boston.

The mayor's plan included a three-year interim zoning proposal called the Interim Planning Overlay District. This imposed dramatic new height restrictions throughout the downtown area to give the city time to develop new permanent zoning regulations for separate downtown districts. The mayor's plan also introduced a program to pair the development of prime downtown sites owned by the city with less desirable city-owned neighborhood sites in a parcel-to-parcel linkage program to stimulate neighborhood revitalization. Finally, the plan included new design review requirements as part of the development process. The ambitious nature of A Plan to Manage Growth warrants a closer look.

Interim Planning Overlay District (IPOD). The IPOD was the key to Boston's new downtown growth management program. It was the result of two-and-a-half years of consultation and negotiation that had taken place behind the scenes between the Boston Redevelopment Authority staff and a wide range of interests including developers, neighborhoods, preservationists, open-space advocates and others. In recent years the approach of the BRA in this and other matters has been to build as much consensus as possible around a proposal—whether it be the new zoning proposal or a project approval—before it is brought forward. In the case of the IPOD this worked extremely well. When the proposal was finally presented for adoption in 1987, just weeks after the mayor introduced his comprehensive program, it passed easily. The city had done its homework and set forth a clear need and purpose for the interim zoning. All the behind-the-scenes negotiations had built a constituency for the IPOD with no serious challenges.

The foundation of the IPOD ordinance was a dramatic height restriction imposed across the city. While the height restriction was described in the plan as a return to the 155-foot height limit that existed before 1964, in fact, the new height limits established in various parts of the city varied considerably, with limits set well below 155 feet in most areas. The IPOD ordinance established four types of subdistricts—priority preservation subdistricts, restricted growth subdistricts, medium growth subdistricts and economic development subdistricts—with height restrictions based on the character of existing buildings and the current land uses in the districts. The limits ranged from 40 feet with floor area ratios of 2:1 permitted in certain priority preservation subdistricts, to heights of 300 feet with permitted floor area ratios of 14:1 in the two economic development area subdistricts.

Accompanying what amounted to a comprehensive downzoning of the downtown area were a number of provisions allowing for larger development projects included in the IPOD. There are provisions in all except the priority preservation subdistricts for specifically defined "enhanced" height and density allowances. To qualify for these enhanced height and density allowances, the developer must demonstrate that the additional size of a building would be compatible with its surroundings, is not a rooftop addition to a historic building, and that the public benefits outweigh any burdens imposed. In the economic development subdistricts, projects must also meet special design review requirements and provide adequate child care for the development's employees to be allowed to build to these greater height and density limits.

In addition to these enhanced height and density provisions, the IPOD allows developers to apply for the designation of Planned Development Area for a project if it is located within one of a few small designated areas. With design review, developments in a Planned Development Area are permitted to go as high as 400 feet. This provision was one of the ways the BRA put together consensus around the interim ordinance. By allowing this option, it was able to provide for major development plans already in the works, but not actually under way, when the new ordinance was adopted.

What the IPOD provides, despite the various options for gaining a limited amount of additional height and density, is a substantial reduction in the size building owners are allowed to construct on most sites and in most districts in the city. This relieves a significant amount of development pressure from existing buildings and neighborhoods. Critics argue there is still a great deal of room for negotiation through the various exceptions allowed and the design review process, and this is certainly the case. On balance, however, most people seem to agree the height limits will have a real effect and will lower the profile of the Boston skyline substantially in coming years.

Linkage Programs. A second major element in the plan was one of the most innovative and extensive linkage programs in the country. Linkage policies are designed to take a portion of value created by investment in areas undergoing substantial development and direct that value to provide affordable housing or other public benefits throughout a city. This concept was first initiated in San Francisco, and Boston adopted its first linkage requirement in 1983. Developers of office buildings were required to pay $5 a square foot for every new square foot of space constructed beyond a threshold of 100,000 square feet. Unlike San Francisco, where the entire linkage payment was required at the time of construction, in Boston the linkage fee was initially prorated over a 12-year period. In 1985 the prorated period was shortened to seven years. As of January 1988, 32 major developments were committed to pay some $45 million in housing linkage payments. In 1986 the city added another $1 per square foot for every square foot constructed over the threshold of 100,000 square feet. This additional $1 was to pay for job training programs for Boston residents, so local citizens could capture a larger share of the new jobs being generated.

In addition to the affordable housing and jobs linkage program, as part of the plan, Boston also developed a unique program called "parcel-to-parcel linkage," to extend downtown investment interest into the city's less economically healthy neighborhoods. To accomplish this, the Boston Redevelopment Authority pairs parcels of property it owns in the hot market of downtown real estate with parcels it owns in neighborhoods. It then requires a developer who wants to purchase the downtown parcel to purchase and develop a neighborhood parcel as well. It is one of the most ambitious efforts yet by a city to stretch the benefits of downtown development to outlying neighborhoods.

Development Review Requirements. Another important aspect of the Plan to Manage Growth was a strengthening of the Boston Redevelopment Authority's review powers and the addition of a new design review body, the Boston Civic Design Commission.

This portion of the plan was implemented in a January 1988 amendment to the zoning ordinance in which the new development review process was set out in detail. In addition to the usual concerns of a planning review process such as parking, access and construction management, there are several specific requirements of interest to preservationists. There are environmental review requirements related to wind, shadow, glare and other impacts on adjacent buildings and the environment. There is also a requirement that an applicant submit an analysis that "sets forth measures intended to minimize or mitigate any potential adverse effect which the proposed project may have on any historical resources listed in the State Register of Historic Places." This in effect establishes a requirement for all local projects that is akin to the Section 106 review process required by the national preservation law when a federally funded project may have a negative impact on historic resources.

In addition to the design reviews carried out by the Boston Redevelopment Authority, all "significant" projects must be reviewed by the 11-member Boston Civic Design Commission, a newly constituted body appointed by the mayor. Developments considered significant are those more than six stories high or in the vicinity of parks and historic buildings. The commission has the power to recommend to the mayor or the BRA that the design of any significant project be modified. The commission is also charged with assisting the BRA in developing the plans and design guidelines for individual zoning districts. While the commission's jurisdiction is only advisory, the stature of its members (the commission is chaired by the dean of the School of Architecture at MIT), along with its power to hold public hearings, means this can be an important avenue for public influence in the development approval process.

Midtown Cultural District

While the Interim Planning Overlay District set up the overall framework for the revision of Boston's outdated zoning ordinance, it was a first, not a final step. The idea was to get interim zoning in place while the city turned to the task of developing more detailed district-by-district zoning for major areas of the city. A Plan to Manage Growth called for developing district zoning for 11 separate districts. One of the first districts for which permanent regulations have been developed is the Midtown Cultural District.

The area in Boston known as Midtown has a unique location and a checkered history. To the north is the city's extraordinarily successful financial district. To the west is Boston's famous Common and Public Garden. To the east is Chinatown and to the south the Bay Village residential area. While apparently well positioned, Midtown has received little of Boston's recent development activity, which has been concentrated in the financial district, along the waterfront and around the Prudential Center and Copley Square.

Midtown is home to Washington Street, one of this country's most successful downtown retail areas, anchored as it has been for decades by the city's two major department stores—Jordan Marsh and Filene's. It is also home to most of Boston's large old theaters. In the 1950s and 1960s Midtown began to see a number of adult entertainment establishments spring up. In an attempt to keep them from spreading, the city established an adult entertainment area, dubbed the Combat Zone, which it has been trying quietly to eliminate in recent years.

Today, Midtown contains a mixture of retail establishments, large old theaters, boarded-up buildings and a number of significant landmarks. It also has the prospect of two multimillion-dollar mixed-use developments that have received all their development approvals and will proceed, assuming market conditions continue to be favorable. The goals set for this district were to capture the next wave of downtown development and use that private investment to gain such public benefits as new performing arts space, day-care facilities, preservation of historic buildings and housing linkage payments.

Even in a city known for its high level of citizen involvement, the process used to develop the Midtown zoning was ambitious. The concept for the district, as a centralized and revitalized arts and entertainment district adjacent to the major financial area, was the result of a citizen initiative. ARTS Boston, an umbrella group representing dozens of visual and performing arts groups in the city, saw the city's economic boom and new planning endeavors as a major opportunity for the arts. With the support of the mayor's commissioner for the arts, it convinced the Boston Redevelopment Authority to designate the area the Midtown Cultural District. The district was described in the introduction to The Midtown Cultural District Plan:

> The Midtown Cultural District Plan has been developed to guide the reemergence of Midtown Boston as a center of commerce, culture, and city life. The district stretches from the edges of Boston Common to Downtown Crossing, the Combat Zone, the Theater District, and Park Square. The area has many unique characteristics including a long history as the region's center for theater and retailing. It is centrally located in the middle of downtown Boston's thriving residential and business communities. Yet, the district also contains a high concentration of vacant land and underutilized historic buildings. This combination makes Midtown an ideal place for revitalization as a vibrant mixed-use district, with new and existing cultural facilities, offices, shops, and restaurants in new and renovated buildings.

What followed the delineation of this district in 1987 was two years of intense negotiations between arts enthusiasts, developers, preservationists, neighborhood people and BRA staff over land uses, densities and a host of other issues that eventually translated into new zoning for the Midtown District.

The city set up a citizen planning body known as the Midtown Cultural District Task Force. It was chaired by the energetic head of ARTS Boston and was open to all comers. The group was quite large initially but settled down finally to include developers, strong arts representation and dedicated participants from the preservation and open-space communities. Day-care interests were well represented by city staff. Neighborhood advocates came and went. Formal task force meetings, which were staffed by the BRA, were accompanied by many small meetings between the various interests and BRA staff. This collaborative planning effort allowed all groups to exchange views and see where their goals and priorities converged.

While developers and many citizens would have preferred to end up with a code stating clearly what could be built and what could not, BRA staff felt it was necessary to preserve some flexibility to balance various interests on a project-by-project basis. What emerged was a complex set of rules with a variety of opportunities for negotiation, although this system remained within the overall context of the significant height restrictions established in the Interim Planning Overlay District.

Major provisions governing the Midtown District include:

- Significantly lower height limits on the borders of the Common and the Public Garden and in established neighborhoods;

- Some increased height and density allowances in certain areas if neighborhood businesses, on-site day care, substantially rehabilitated theaters, community service organizations or certain other ground-level uses are provided;

- Provisions for large-scale developments within three Planned Development Areas with requirements that the developer provide one or more of the following: a new theater or cultural facility, substantial rehabilitation of a historic building or an existing theater, or some affordable housing.

Preservationists can cite several victories in the Midtown process and product. Height limits of 65 to 125 feet in some areas alone will probably be sufficient to protect buildings within the four protection areas. In addition, substantial rehabilitation of a historic building is one of the public benefits a developer can offer to secure approval for a Planned Development Area. Substantial rehabilitation of theaters—some of which are historic—allows a developer to qualify for increased height and density. Detailed design and environmental reviews dealing with everything from facades, light and shadow, and other impacts on existing buildings provide additional protection for historic structures. In 1981, through the efforts of the Boston Landmarks Commission, much of what is now known as the Midtown Cultural District was listed in the National Register of Historic Places. However, National Register listing provides no real protection for historic resources. In contrast to local landmark designations, such listing merely subjects federally assisted projects affecting historic buildings to a review and consultation process. Because only a few of the Midtown District's historic structures are locally designated protected landmarks, Boston may be viewed as a test to see how well the undesignated historic buildings fare under a zoning ordinance designed to alleviate development pressures that threaten them.

During the Midtown Cultural District negotiation process, preservationists learned that preservation and arts, though often linked, do not necessarily converge. Preservationists had hoped to form an alliance to save some of the area's old theaters. They discovered, however, that the arts community viewed the best of these theaters as safe because they had their own constituencies. Arts advocates regarded other theaters as white elephants and as a drain on their coffers. They saw a need for smaller, more versatile space, not the huge old theaters of the past. In many ways, preservationists found greater affinity with urban design and open-space advocates for whom scale, views and visual attractiveness were major concerns.

Specific Preservation Initiatives

Preservation values were acknowledged and incorporated throughout A Plan to Manage Growth. In addition to the various zoning and design review changes we have reviewed, the plan also proposed an ambitious preservation amendment to the zoning code. It was intended to give interim protection to hundreds of buildings of national, state and local significance until more permanent protection could be established by landmark designation.

The city of Boston has had a local preservation law and landmarks commission since 1975. Appointed by the mayor and approved by the city council, the commission consists of nine individuals and nine alternates from the architecture, preservation, real estate and business communities. The commission has the usual responsibilities of inventorying historic properties in the city, preparing study reports for designation, designating landmarks and districts, overseeing design review and granting certificates of appropriateness. The mayor has 15 days in which to approve or disapprove a designation by the commission and the city council has an additional 30 days to consider overriding a designation approved by the mayor.

An unusual feature in Boston's preservation law—one that is particularly troubling to preservationists—seriously inhibits the ability to designate downtown historic districts. The state enabling legislation for Boston's ordinance requires a different procedure for designating downtown districts from that required to designate individual landmarks or districts outside the downtown area. In general, the Boston ordinance requires a majority vote by the landmarks commission to designate a property or district. The mayor then has 15 days in which to approve or disapprove the designation and the city council has an additional 30 days to override, by a two-thirds vote, any designation made by the mayor. In the case of downtown historic districts, designations can only be made by a two-thirds vote of the city council, a difficult consensus to achieve. At present there are no local historic districts in the commercial section of downtown and only three neighborhood historic districts in the entire downtown area. It appears Boston will have to rely primarily on individual landmark designations to protect its downtown historic resources.

As of April 1990, the city had 56 designated landmarks citywide. Originally the landmarks commission was staffed by the BRA, but it has been moved into the Environment Department with other conservation activities. The commission staff is not large enough to keep pace with the large number of properties petitioned for designation, and many historic resources eligible for designation have been left unprotected. An amendment seeking to remedy this situation was proposed as part of A Plan to Manage Growth to provide five years of interim protection for more than 200 buildings of national, state or local significance throughout the city. It also would have included interim protection for eligible districts. The amendment, a supplement to preservation laws already in place, was to protect "potentially significant" buildings from development or demolition while the Boston Landmarks Commission had time to prepare documentation and seek permanent protection for these resources.

The amendment was introduced before the city zoning commission in October 1987 with the strong support of the Boston Preservation Alliance, the city's major preservation advocacy group. The alliance believed that the direct protection the preservation amendment would provide for historic buildings was key to an effective downtown preservation program. Property owners and developers expressed the usual concerns about five years of interim protection for all buildings deemed to be eligible for protection but not yet officially designated as historic. They argued it would provide automatic protection without requiring buildings to meet the test of the designation process, suggesting quietly this might be considered a taking of private property without due process or just compensation.

The Boston Landmarks Commission publicly supported study of the amendment. The commission was in charge of analyzing the amendment for the city and it acted cautiously throughout the debate. The commission's citywide survey of historic resources is about 75 percent complete and the commission believes it is moving as quickly as it can on designation. Without the addition of new staff, the pressure to prepare study reports on all eligible properties within the five-year period would have placed great stress on the office. It might have forced some organizational decisions about how to get help and whether or not to move the commission back into the Boston Redevelopment Authority. Concerns were raised about the commission's independence from the rest of the development decision process if some of these organizational changes were made.

Following almost two years of debate, the preservation amendment was defeated. The leadership of the Boston Preservation Alliance and other preservationists are very concerned about this defeat and the ongoing lack of protection for many of Boston's most valuable historic resources.

Conclusion

Boston's preservation laws are much like those found in cities across the country—with the important exception of the legislative hurdles designed to restrict designation of downtown districts. Once designated, buildings in Boston have considerable protection, but designation is a difficult process and many eligible resources have not yet been proposed due to staffing limitations at the Boston Landmarks Commission.

Preservation was articulated as a primary goal of the ambitious growth management plan initiated in Boston, but attempts to strengthen the protection of historic landmarks through the proposed preservation amendment were unsuccessful. Many buildings eligible for protection are vulnerable while they wait for the time-consuming process of nomination and designation. In the meantime, it remains to be seen whether the rest of Boston's growth management plan—height limits, rehabilitation incentives and design review—will be sufficient without landmark or historic district designation to protect a significant portion of the city's historic fabric and buildings.

References

Development Review Procedures. City of Boston, Boston Redevelopment Authority, 1986.

Downtown Zoning: Midtown Cultural District. Plan to Manage Growth. City of Boston, Boston Redevelopment Authority, 1989.

A Plan to Manage Growth. City of Boston, Boston Redevelopment Authority, 1987.

Aerial view of Cincinnati. (Elder Photographic/Cincinnati Convention and Visitors Bureau)

Cincinnati

In the coming decade, Cincinnati, Ohio, is likely to see some conflict over two major goals it has set for its downtown area: attraction of new office development and preservation of existing historic buildings. Up to this point these goals have survived side by side, but most vacant and underused land in the downtown area is now developed and pressure is shifting to sites occupied by late 19th- and early 20th-century buildings.

During the 1980s, Cincinnati government, business and preservation leaders worked together to develop the Cincinnati 2000 Plan. This plan set goals for new development designed to boost the city's economy. It also identified historic resources in the city's central core and gave considerable attention to the importance of protecting these. As the city council considered a series of steps to implement the Cincinnati 2000 Plan, choices that do not bode well for downtown historic buildings were made to lessen the conflict between the two goals of economic development and historic preservation.

In adopting a new zoning ordinance to implement the plan, the city settled on generous building height and density allowances to stimulate new development. It also adopted an extensive bonus system allowing even greater densities in exchange for a variety of public benefits. In an attempt to reconcile preservation and new development, the city made the preservation of historic buildings one of the public benefits developers could provide in exchange for constructing larger buildings. However, many people believe the heights and densities permitted without bonuses are already so generous that most bonus provisions will never be used.

As part of the implementation program, preservationists also attempted to get landmark designation for several valuable historic buildings in the downtown core. They were turned down when property owners convinced the city council this would place undue restrictions on future development.

Cincinnati has a historic preservation ordinance and a long history of neighborhood preservation, but a review of recent actions suggests that historic resources in the downtown area may not fare as well. With no landmark protection for a large number of historic buildings and generous height and density allowances for new buildings, downtown landmarks in Cincinnati will need to depend primarily on their economic value for survival for the foreseeable future.

The City

Settled by pioneers on the northern shores of the Ohio River, in its early days Cincinnati enjoyed a lively steamboat trade. Pork was a major product, raised in the surrounding agricultural region and shipped down river leading to the early nickname "Porkopolis." Cincinnati has also been called the Queen of the West and the Blue Chip City—descriptions that suggest charm and a place where it's good to do business. Led by the multibillion-dollar Procter and Gamble Company, which began making candles from the byproducts of the pork rendering process, Cincinnati is home to 12 Fortune 500 companies. The first families of Cincinnati provide generous support to the local art museums, symphony and ballet, allowing Cincinnati to boast rich cultural offerings for a city of its size.

Like all cities, Cincinnati has experienced its share of economic ups and downs. During the 1940s and 1950s, the city languished as many of the old manufacturing businesses moved or closed downtown and people moved out. Cincinnatians date the beginning of the city's current revitalization to the decision in the early 1960s to locate the new stadium on the riverfront adjacent to the central business district, rather than in the suburbs to the north. Riverfront Stadium, completed in 1970, combined with other urban renewal efforts, led to the first wave of new downtown office building in Cincinnati in decades.

Cincinnati is a relatively compact city of 78 square miles. It has firm natural boundaries in the river to the south and a ring of hills to the north. Substantially developed by 1900, Cincinnati has a wealth of historic resources including many attractive neighborhoods and an impressive collection of late 19th- and early 20th-century office buildings in the heart of the central business district. The most imposing of these is the 49-story Carew Tower. Built during the height of the Depression by a wealthy Cincinnati family, Carew Tower was the first mixed-use office, retail, hotel building in the country, preceding Rockefeller Center by several years. As the city's tallest building, the tower has dominated the Cincinnati skyline for more than 50 years. It stands as a monument to the pride and confidence Cincinnati's citizens have had in their city even in the bleakest of economic times.

Since 1980 Cincinnati has experienced a steady addition of one or two major new office structures a year. Like most cities, Cincinnati is working hard to strengthen its downtown retail sector and add more housing and

Historic Fountain Square, located in the heart of downtown Cincinnati. (Cincinnati Convention and Visitors Bureau)

cultural activities to the downtown mix. The city is pleased with the strength of its economy during the 1980s, but government and business interests continue to take a very aggressive posture toward attracting new business.

Over the last 30 years, city government has played a very active role in downtown development and redevelopment. Cincinnati did not experience the extensive clearance programs carried out in many cities that left large tracts of undeveloped land. Its urban renewal efforts have been more of an infill nature with selective clearance and generous use of eminent domain for land assembly purposes. The city's major contributions to the revitalization process have consisted of reduced prices on urban renewal land and, more recently, long-term land leasing combined with generous infrastructure contributions. The latter have included parking structures and a skywalk system connecting major hotel and retail establishments with each other and with the city's newly expanded convention center. The city has also used major public investments such as the stadium, the construction of its widely known public plaza, Fountain Square and the new convention center to stimulate private investment.

As a part of its 1964 urban renewal plan and implementation process, the city adopted a development contract process whereby all projects that involved some kind of city contribution required the developer to sign a contract. The contract included city and developer obligations, including the requirement that such projects submit to design review. The design reviews were conducted by a four-person Urban Design Review Board appointed by the city manager and convened at the request of the director of economic development to review individual projects. In reviewing projects the board used the basic guidance of a 1964 Urban Design Plan developed as part of the 1964 Urban Renewal Plan. This process of negotiated development under the direction of the city manager and the director of economic development served for many years as a substitute for a badly outdated zoning code.

Cincinnati 2000 Plan

The most recent era in downtown planning in Cincinnati began in 1979. One of the first cities to adopt a comprehensive plan in the 1920s, Cincinnati has prided itself on being a city that develops long-range plans and sticks to them. In 1964, as part of its urban renewal effort, Cincinnati developed a plan for its central business district that emphasized the development of commercial, office and hotel space. By the late 1970s the recommendations contained in that plan had been implemented—new office buildings were in place, skywalks connected hotels with the convention center and retail space—and the city decided it was time to create a new vision and plan.

The planning process began when the city manager convened a Working Review Committee made up of four members of the city council, the city manager, the planning director, the economic development director and 14 representatives of the community including both business leaders and preservation advocates. As with the 1964 plan, a business committee, made up of the chief executive officers of the city's largest corporations, and the Chamber of Commerce took a major role in initiating and developing the plan. Much of the work was done in subcommittees and substantial citizen input was sought with the help of a planning consultant. The plan was completed in a year and adopted by the city council in 1982. It has received only minor revisions since then.

The goals and recommendations contained in the Cincinnati 2000 Plan reflect the city's concern with new downtown development. The plan calls for additional office development; expansion of retail activity, particularly specialty shops and services; new downtown housing; an entertainment and cultural district; and an expanded convention center. Dividing the central business district into sectors, it proposes the type and intensity of development appropriate for each sector, including land uses, height limits and densities. The overall approach calls for a pyramid, with the highest height limits and densities in the central core around Fountain Square and south toward the river, and a stepping down to the north, east and west as one moves out toward the neighborhoods.

The plan strongly encourages additional growth and development in the downtown area but seeks to expand the diversity of uses and activities brought by that growth. It emphasizes respect for historic resources and the need to set strict design guidelines for all new development. There are special sections in the plan dealing with auto and pedestrian access, open-space improvements, parking, lighting and streetscapes, and historic and architectural resources. It acknowledges that "a preservation program is an integral part of the Cincinnati 2000 Plan." It identifies all the historic resources in the downtown area and recommends that several National Register districts on the edges of the downtown area receive local protection. The plan acknowledges the presence of an unusual concentration of valuable historic resources along Fourth Street. It notes:

> A number of historic resources are found along Fourth Street from Race to Main. These historic resources should be preserved. A local historic district should be considered as one of several options for preserving these resources. In addition, the special scale of Fourth Street should be preserved. It is the responsibility of the Urban Design Review Board and the Historic Conservation Board to develop guidelines which maintain the historic character and special scale of the Fourth Street streetscapes.

The values and goals of resource protection and good design are found throughout the Cincinnati 2000 Plan, but some inherent conflicts exist in the document. The same area that the city sees as the most logical for the next round of intense office construction—in the central core and south toward the riverfront—contains the Fourth Street corridor, site of many of the city's most valuable historic resources. As might have been expected, these conflicts came to the fore as the city took steps to implement the plan.

Zoning Ordinance

The central element in the implementation of the Cincinnati 2000 Plan was a complete reworking of the city's zoning code, which had not been revised substantially since 1963. The question before the city was how far did it want to go in translating the specific goals and recommendations included in the plan into the zoning ordinance? The process used to lead up to a city council decision on this matter was the appointment of a special zoning committee and a citizen advisory group to consider various issues and options. The city engaged nationally recognized experts in incentive zoning and design review to prepare background papers and advise them throughout the process. The most sensitive issues addressed were:

- What kinds of bonuses or incentives were called for to implement the plan?

- What kinds of height limits and densities would be allowed by right and how would they affect any bonus plan?

- Should urban design guidelines and review procedures be an official part of the code or kept as part of a less formal negotiation process?

The business community and the city's Office of Economic Development favored generous height and density allowances and the existing, less formal design review requirements to sustain a climate that would be attractive to new development. Others specifically concerned with urban design features, downtown housing, preservation, day care, public art and other elements favored lower height limits and a more formal design review process to increase the city's leverage. The consultants argued that lower height and density allowances would be the most effective way for the city to achieve the vision of Cincinnati presented in the plan:

> The critical consideration here is that the height and floor area ratio (FAR) permitted without benefit of bonuses must be set sufficiently below the maximums established on the maps such that developers will have an incentive to provide identified public benefits in exchange for the increase in construction area needed to reach the upper limit of the particular limit and FAR standards allowed in a district.

When it was finally adopted in 1987, the zoning amendment included an elaborate bonus system with incentives for skywalk atriums, for stepping buildings back as they go up from the street level, and for bus shelters, day care, plazas, gardens, housing, skywalks, arcades, public art, underground parking and historic preservation. There are some requirements built into the code, such as first-floor retail space on certain blocks, but in general the city is expecting the bonus system to deliver the desired public benefits. Certain benefits, such as day-care facilities, may be provided voluntarily because potential tenants demand them.

The ordinance established no height limits immediately around Fountain Square and a uniform height limit of approximately 500 feet (phrased as 1,050 feet above sea level) for the remaining 25-block core of the downtown area. This represented a fairly significant departure from the Cincinnati 2000 Plan, which had proposed height limits even around Fountain

Square that stepped down fairly rapidly as one moved beyond the blocks immediately surrounding the square. Design guidelines and review were not incorporated into the zoning code and the design review process continues to operate out of the Office of Economic Development as it has for the last 25 years.

Overall the interests of preservationists were much more successfully integrated into the plan than into the zoning ordinance. The plan had called for new high-density development in areas where there were key historic resources, but it had also called for a careful balancing of design and conservation concerns with new development. The height and density limits established by the zoning ordinance intensified the potential conflicts. In addition, the development rights granted under the zoning ordinance are generous enough that many people believe developers will have no incentive to seek the bonuses for preservation and other public benefits.

Preservation Successes

Historic preservation has experienced a number of successes in Cincinnati in recent years. These include the $28 million renovation of the Netherland Hotel, a 1930s Art Deco masterpiece that is part of the Carew Tower complex adjacent to Fountain Square; a $50-million, bond-financed restoration of the Union Terminal building, which will be used as a home for the Cincinnati Historical Society and the Museum of Natural History; and the restoration of Findlay Market, one of Cincinnati's great open-air markets. Between 1981 and 1985, 136 projects were completed with the help of the federal tax credits available to encourage rehabilitation of historic buildings. This resulted in a total of $141 million in rehabilitation investment.

The single most significant accomplishment in preservation in Cincinnati over the last decade was the passage of the city's local preservation ordinance in 1980. The Cincinnati ordinance provides that when the city council designates a historic district, structure or site, it will also adopt conservation guidelines for that particular district, structure or site.

> Section 741.11. Insofar as practicable, the conservation guidelines shall promote redevelopment of historic structures and compatible new development within historic districts. The guidelines shall not limit new construction within an historic site or district to any one period or architectural style but shall seek to preserve the integrity of existing historic structures. The conservation guidelines shall take into account the impact of the designation of a structure, site, or district on the residents of the affected area, the effect of the designation on the economic and social characteristics of the affected area, the projected impact of the designation on the budget of the city, as well as the factors listed in Section 741.7(c).

The ordinance is administered by a nine-member board, appointed by the city manager, whose members consist of two architects, a preservationist, a historian, an attorney, a real estate developer and three community representatives. The Historic Conservation Board has a staff directed by an urban conservator who serves as secretary to the board and as assistant to the director of city planning. The Historic Conservation Board has the power to nominate properties for historic designation, prepare conservation guidelines and grant or deny requests to alter or demolish historic properties. The board is also able to accept easements, although little use has been made of this provision. Appeals of any board decisions are made to the city council.

The Cincinnati ordinance includes a number of important provisions, which give it additional strength. Designated historic districts are overlay districts—that is, superimposed over existing zoning rules and regulations—but they are also integrated into the text and map of the zoning ordinance. The Historic Conservation Board is authorized to grant conditional use permits or variances dealing with such matters as lot coverage, yard requirements, building heights, parking, fences and landscaping in order to encourage the preservation of historic buildings. Modifications proposed by the board supersede the conditions in the underlying zone.

> Section 3501.1. The provisions of this chapter shall control and supersede wherever inconsistent with other existing provisions of the zoning code, all regulations of the underlying zone district, and the Cincinnati municipal code.

It should be noted, however, that the board has rarely dealt with questions of land use.

Objections to these changes can be appealed to the city council.

The ordinance provides that certificates of appropriateness—prerequisites for demolishing or altering a historic structure or building a new one in a historic district—are to be denied if a proposal does not conform with the conservation guidelines for that site or district. The only exception to this is when "no feasible and prudent alternative" exists and strict application of the guidelines would deny the owner an opportunity for a reasonable rate of return from his investment in the property, as determined by the Historic Conservation Board. All rules apply to property owned by nonprofit as well as profit-making organizations. In cases where demolition permission must be granted, there are provisions for a 180-day demolition delay while the board explores alternatives. There is also a minimum maintenance requirement to prevent demolition by neglect, although this has never been exercised.

In addition to the 1980 historic preservation ordinance, there are several other pieces of legislation of particular interest with regard to resource conservation in Cincinnati. One is the provision for interim development controls in the city, which can be imposed for a 90-day period and extended up to one year while additional land-use controls of any kind are being considered. This can be invoked by the city council to protect specific areas while they are being studied for designation and is in addition to the 180-day demolition delay for designated structures provided in the preservation ordinance.

Another interesting law provides for the designation of Environmental Quality (EQ) districts. Originally designed to protect the environmentally sensitive hillsides that surround the city to the north, EQ districts are overlay districts that require environmentally compatible development in sensitive areas. Several kinds of EQ districts are permitted, including hillside areas, high public investment areas and areas with specific urban design considerations relating to such things as heights and views. Like historic districts, EQ districts provide the city with a mechanism for reviewing new development. Also, as with historic districts, the city can alter underlying zoning provisions in order to establish an EQ district to protect the character of certain sensitive areas or neighborhoods.

On another level, Cincinnati's zoning ordinance requires landscaping on any lot in the downtown district that is kept vacant for more than 180 days following the demolition of a building. The landscaping must be completed in accordance with a plan approved by the city's planning director. This provision helps the city avoid the problem of having historic or other existing buildings demolished and replaced by untended vacant lots.

All of these laws are important elements in Cincinnati's attempts to protect its resources and the quality of the environment in the center city. Since adopting its preservation ordinance in 1980, Cincinnati has conferred historic designation on 17 local districts and 30 individual structures for a total of approximately 1,230 buildings, an impressive achievement in less than nine years. It has been less successful thus far in providing protection for historic resources in the heart of downtown. While six historic districts and 250 designated landmarks are in the downtown area, they do not include many of the most valuable structures in the city, particularly in the historic Fourth Street area, but not for lack of trying.

Fourth Street Initiative

Fourth Street was Cincinnati's original Main Street. In the 1850s the Broadway of Cincinnati contained residences, quality retail stores and opera houses. During the late 19th and early 20th centuries, Fourth Street became the city's financial district. Four Daniel Burnham office buildings, the world's first reinforced-concrete skyscraper and Cass Gilbert's Central Trust Tower, which, when it was built in 1913, was the world's fifth tallest building, were all added to the streetscape.

Fourth Street has changed very little in the last 50 years. As major new development has taken place along Fifth Street one block north, Fourth

Street has stayed essentially intact. Some substantial rehabilitation has taken place, some vacant parcels exist, and most buildings are reasonably well-used, although a few are boarded up obviously awaiting change. As appropriate development sites on Fifth Street become scarce, the pressure is shifting to Fourth Street.

In an attempt to head off some of the inevitable conflicts between preservation and new development along Fourth Street set up by the Cincinnati 2000 Plan and the new zoning ordinance, the city's urban conservator and Historic Conservation Board hired a consulting firm to help in developing a Fourth Street strategy. In the introduction to a report, entitled "Fourth Street: A Bridge to the Future," the challenge was expressed as follows:

> These two views—Fourth Street as a historic and architectural treasure that should be preserved for future generations, and Fourth Street as an under-developed resource needed for future generations' growth and expansion—present instant controversy to those public and private decisionmakers whose actions will determine the future of the street. The dilemma is heightened by the fact that Third Street—where major development parcels do exist—is seen as being outside the desirable central core. Fourth Street, elevated 20 to 25 feet above Third, is the southernmost active, pedestrian street in the core. In this way, Fourth Street acts as a physical and psychological terminus to development and is thus a barrier to an expanded downtown.

The concept developed to address this dilemma was to use Fourth Street as a "bridge" to available land on Third Street. The report proposed that historic buildings on Fourth Street be preserved and serve as entrances to new large buildings on Third Street. It called for several levels of structured parking beneath Third Street buildings in order to raise them to Fourth Street level. With selective demolition and substantial renovation of Fourth Street structures, it was suggested that imaginative connections could be made by creating shopping arcades, entry gardens and interior walkways directly from Fourth Street to Third Street buildings. Instead of serving as a barrier, Fourth Street would thus become the catalyst for development of Third Street, allowing the apparently conflicting goals of preservation and new downtown development to be met.

To accomplish the plan, the Historic Conservation Board recommended designation of a Fourth Street Historic District. To make the proposal compatible with the dual goals of facilitating new development and preserving existing structures, the plan recommended the adoption of a number of special provisions. The most significant related to the circumstances under which buildings could be demolished. In addition to the basic conditions under which demolition is generally permitted, including public safety and economic hardship, the plan recommended approving

13 noncontributing buildings outright for demolition. Secondly and far more radically, the plan proposed permitting any historic building to be demolished for new development—even if a reasonable rate of return is available—if the project would result in the rehabilitation of other historic structures or allow a significant project to be built at the rear of historic buildings. In all cases, 75 percent of each block, on both sides of the street, would have had to be retained so the scale and historic character would not be altered. These additional demolition conditions were accompanied by recommendations for streamlined review guidelines; a provision for the Urban Design Review Board to provide advisory comment to the Historic Conservation Board on all new construction in the district; and a provision to allow a transfer of development rights to adjacent sites.

Despite the effort that went into accommodating conflicting interests, when the proposal was brought forward for public comment, there was strong resistance from the business community. Business leaders were concerned about the loss of flexibility in what could be built in the city's next prime development area. Sensing the strength of the resistance, preservationists never actually proposed Fourth Street for historic district designation but instead sought protection for the most valuable structures as individual landmarks. When these buildings came before the city council for a vote, the nominations were tabled indefinitely. While preservationists succeeded in getting a much smaller area on the western end of Fourth Street designated as a local district, the council's action left most of the historic buildings on Fourth Street without any local protection.

The case for protecting the historic resources on Fourth Street was made almost exclusively by the Historic Conservation Board and its staff. The Miami Purchase Association, the major preservation advocacy group in the area, did not attempt to play a major role in downtown preservation issues. Although the association has since become more involved in downtown development issues, during this period it focused most of its attention on neighborhood and county issues, where it saw the greatest need and the greatest potential gains. The association entered the Fourth Street debate when the conservation board proposed several Fourth Street buildings for individual landmark protection. At this point, the Miami Purchase Association came forward and endorsed a full historic district, saying the resources warranted this and hoping this would at the very least strengthen the Conservation Board's more modest proposal for individual building protection. The strategy did not work. The city's economic development department and major property owners on Fourth Street who wanted to keep the doors open to a variety of development possibilities were unwilling to allow historic building protections limit their options.

Up to this point little has been demolished on Fourth Street, although one whole block that houses the Dixie Terminal building with its dramatic two-story glass and marble arcade appears to be in danger. Several important buildings have undergone substantial rehabilitation, a development that should improve their prospects for survival for a number of years. The idea of building new structures on Third Street with entrances on the Fourth Street level and structured parking underneath has already been accepted but not in connection with using or saving any historic structures. The future of Fourth Street is unclear. There will almost certainly be some redevelopment and, given the new zoning, it is likely to be substantial in size. Whether particular buildings will be saved will depend on some combination of their perceived value, the problems they create for land assembly and larger scale development, and overall market forces in Cincinnati. Very little in the city's current regulatory scheme is likely to affect this significantly.

Conclusion

A number of factors appear to have contributed to the decisions reached in Cincinnati regarding height limits, design review and historic resource protection on Fourth Street. The city is fairly small and has not experienced the kind of growth that leads to citizen uprisings in response to traffic and the loss of sunlight, views, human scale and historic fabric. Cincinnati as a city is still basically pro-growth. The constituency favoring development constraints to ensure historic preservation in downtown Cincinnati was not large enough or vocal enough to outweigh business and economic development concerns. The "bridge" proposal put forward for Fourth Street was an attempt to reconcile preservation with goals for new development downtown. But if historic district or structure designation had been granted on Fourth Street, considerable power over development decisions in that area would have been transferred from the city manager and the director of economic development to the Historic Conservation Board. It would have represented a major shift in power over downtown development decisions—one that Cincinnati was not prepared to make at the time.

References

Cincinnati 2000: A Comprehensive Development Plan for Downtown. October 1, 1984, modified November 3, 1986.

"Fourth Street: A Bridge to the Future." A Conservation/Development Design Plan. Cincinnati City Planning Department, Cincinnati Historic Conservation Board, October 1985.

Planning and Legal Framework for Implementation of the Cincinnati 2000 Plan. Cincinnati City Planning Department, October 16, 1985.

Denver residents celebrate the opening of their 16th Street transit mall in 1983. (Fred C. Larkin)

Denver

The story of the Lower Downtown Historic District in Denver, Colo., is one of politics, conflict, compromises and mayoral leadership. The district's creation took more than a decade of dedicated effort by the local preservation community against a constantly changing political and economic background. Today, preservation activists are still working hard to see that the package of landmark protection, design controls, civic improvements and business investment they fought so hard to get for the historic district is fully implemented.

Although Denver's preservationists ultimately realized their major objectives, this case study illustrates the challenge of political action and negotiation.

The story of the Lower Downtown Historic District, as told by those who participated in its creation, has five major stages.

Stage 1. During the 1970s, preservationists began to identify historic buildings in the Lower Downtown and to build public support for their preservation and the idea of a historic district. This stage involved efforts to publicize the area and to help the public understand that the area had the potential to become a distinctive and important resource to the city.

Stage 2. In 1982 the city amended its zoning ordinance for Lower Downtown to provide incentives for residential development and historic preservation as well as to enliven the area through more street-level pedestrian activity. The ordinance permitted developers to build larger buildings in exchange for the creation of new housing units and the purchase of development rights from historic property owners. However, it failed to include any demolition controls or design standards for new construction. While preservationists considered these essential to any meaningful protection for historic structures, they had agreed to the ordinance expecting that a proposal for design and demolition controls would be submitted soon to the city council. This did not happen.

Stage 3. Between 1984 and 1986 preservationists turned their attention to a collaborative planning process initiated by the mayor to develop a long-range vision for Denver's future downtown development. This phase culminated in May 1986 when the city council endorsed a Downtown Area Plan that included a comprehensive package of recommendations for preserving and revitalizing Lower Downtown.

Stage 4. Following the Downtown Area Plan's adoption, the city council was encouraged to implement the plan's recommendation that Lower Downtown be designated a protected local historic district. Although political support for this recommendation was tenuous at first, the council ultimately approved historic district status for Lower Downtown in March 1988.

Stage 5. Today, Denver has a comprehensive historic preservation program in place in Lower Downtown. Preservationists are now working to see that the various commitments made to the historic district are realized.

This case study will concentrate on Stages 3, 4 and 5 because they are the heart of the Lower Downtown story. However, some brief background is presented from Stages 1 and 2 to provide a context for more recent events.

Lower Downtown

Lower Downtown is a historic warehouse district located at the north end of Denver's 16th Street Mall, bounded by Speer Boulevard and 20th Street, Larimer Square and the Central Platte Valley. It is the city's birth-place and the original location for many of its institutions.

A 25-block area, Lower Downtown represents the largest concentration of urban historic buildings in the Denver region. It contains an interesting mix of offices, shops, restaurants and housing, and it is becoming a center for the arts and design community. Most of the buildings are low in scale and built of orange-red brick. Although they are not necessarily distinctive when considered individually, together they are impressive and present an attractive, cohesive appearance.

The Downtown Area Plan stated that Lower Downtown's special historic character, human scale and architectural detail could become a "market asset to downtown." The plan asserted that the district's historic character was a "pleasure for the whole region to enjoy and share with the world."

That was the vision. Although the area was reviving from the deterioration of the 1970s, when it was described by *Denver Business Journal* as a collection of "old worn-out warehouses, run-down hotels and seedy bars," it had some distance to go. Many people still saw Lower Downtown as only a way over the Platte River or to the central downtown.

Downtown Renewal and Growth

Between 1978 and 1982, Denver downtown real estate boomed as the

Market Center in the Lower Downtown Historic District, Denver. To make the development project more feasible, the interiors of these six buildings were combined. The center houses offices of Historic Denver and the historic district's business office. (©1990 Roger Whitacre)

demand for new energy resources throughout the country soared. Denverites joked that the Colorado state bird had become the "construction crane" because it dominated the downtown skyline. Denver's high-rise office structures seemed to multiply overnight. Downtown office towers were filled with more than 1,000 firms, representing oil, uranium, coal and natural gas interests. A feeling that the boom would never end caused property values to ascend dramatically throughout the downtown area. This speculative inflation extended from the office core to the Lower Downtown. Critics of this building boom maintained that Denver was being "Houstonized," just as San Franciscans had decried their "Manhattanization." Like Houston, the other prominent "energy city," Denver later learned the hard way how vulnerable its economy was to the sometimes wild swings in the energy sector.

During this boom period, a strong bond that later proved important developed between the city government and the Denver Partnership, the major downtown business association, through a collaborative effort to revitalize the city's 16th Street Mall.

The 16th Street Mall is a mile-long spine running from the State Capitol and Civic Center to Lower Downtown. Flanked by retail stores, office buildings and civic spaces, it represents Denver's counterattack on suburban malls and their free parking. The success of the city and the Denver Partnership in making 16th Street a downtown centerpiece had bolstered local confidence—an intangible force that nonetheless produced visible effects. The partnership's role in this project had so enhanced the organization's local standing that its support was considered critical to the success of later planning initiatives.

The creation of the 16th Street Mall carried a price: rebuilding was so extensive, Denver lost much of its unique character. To be sure, it still had the mountain setting to give it a sense of place, yet preservationists felt that preserving Lower Downtown was critical to maintaining that sense.

Collaborative Planning

In July 1984 Mayor Federico Pena inaugurated a major downtown planning effort. He appointed 28 civic, business and government leaders to a prestigious steering committee and charged the committee with preparing a Downtown Area Plan to guide Denver into the 21st century. The mayor emphasized that the planning process was to be collaborative. That is, it was to involve all of the major stakeholders in the Denver downtown.

This initiative and the decision to emphasize its collaborative nature reflected the influence of the Denver Partnership, which played a key role throughout the project. Nationally, such organizations as the partnership have pushed private sector involvement in consensus-building, collaborative approaches to downtown planning.

Collaborative planning differs from traditional planning carried out by city government planners in that it gives an important financing, staffing and leadership role to the private sector. Although downtown business and property interests have always been consulted and have been influential in downtown planning, often the formal plans created by city planning officials lack the private sector understanding and commitment they need to work. The nemesis of planning, it has often been noted, is that plans are put on a shelf and never really used as guides for action.

Collaborative planning presents some difficulties, however. It places heavy demands on those involved in the process. Those who are not well represented, or who support goals not as widely accepted as others, can feel co-opted by a plan they did not shape. Since the planning process involves much negotiation, if a party lacks the resources and the skill to participate effectively, its interests may be ignored or overrun. Simply put, collaborative planning involves the play of power and influence in an arena in which not all the parties are equal.

Although preservationists were highly visible on various subcommittees, they were allowed only one member on the downtown steering committee. Their selection was Lisa Purdy, a local preservation activist with experience in real estate development and a good understanding of land-use issues. Because she had a reputation for being willing to confront tough issues and to negotiate hard, she had the confidence of her constituency.

The preservation community understood the importance of the

mayor's collaborative planning effort to the future of historic properties in Lower Downtown. Soon after the mayor's announcement, Historic Denver, Inc., persuaded the Denver Partnership to submit a joint application to the National Trust for Historic Preservation for a Critical Issues Fund grant to help develop a preservation strategy for Lower Downtown. A grant was approved.

Even with the grant, the planning process strained the resources of the preservation organizations and their representatives. There were committees and subcommittees, meetings and more meetings, all of which demanded extensive research and negotiating skills. The preservationists constantly faced arguments and positions that were difficult to counter. Increasingly they recognized the need for strong preparation and coalition building. They often wished for better information resources and data on major historic preservation issues.

But if the collaborative nature of this process was noteworthy, so too was the substantive education of the steering committee members on such issues as urban design, historic preservation and land use. The committee brought national experts in from other parts of the country to meet with committee members and to share information and ideas. Preservationists said later that a presentation made at one of the committee's retreats by Ed Bacon, the nationally known former planning director of Philadelphia, helped greatly to reinforce points they had been trying to make. Other experts contributed similarly to the committee's education and helped to elevate the overall quality of the negotiations and discussions.

In addition to the collaborative nature of this planning effort, its timing was significant. The project took place during a lull in Denver's building boom. Because earlier development pressures had eased, the climate for considering new historic preservation strategies had improved.

Recommendations for Lower Downtown

The highest priority of the preservation community throughout this process was the establishment of Lower Downtown as a local historic district with strong protections.

In 1982, the preservationists' willingness to go along with higher densities for Lower Downtown had rested upon an expectation that property owners would work with them within six months on new design standards for the area. Although this never happened, the earlier relationships established between preservationists and property owners had also helped to generate a mutual interest in taking another look at ways to combine historic preservation with vigorous, but compatible, economic development in this area.

This interest was strengthened by the success of Denver's historic Larimer Square, a nearby collection of renovated historic buildings that had previously demonstrated how historic preservation could help to revitalize a downtown retail area and attract visitors. Lower Downtown was already evolving into a fledgling arts district. It had a few jazz clubs and a "feel" that contrasted with the more conventional character of the 16th Street Mall. It was beginning to be looked upon as a potential source of downtown revitalization rather than as a barrier to high-rise development.

To work for their goal of protecting the historic warehouse district, a number of preservationists volunteered to serve on a special Lower Downtown Task Force created by the steering committee. The task force, which involved more than 90 people, was further subdivided into six work groups concerned with various topics. Over a period of many months, these groups hammered out a set of recommendations for Lower Downtown.

What emerged from these negotiations was a somewhat unsettled outcome, but one with enough agreement on the key points advanced by preservationists that a subcommittee endorsement of them was made to the powerful steering committee. The important elements of that working agreement were that the preservation of the historic character of Lower Downtown was essential; an economic generator and business support function were needed to provide the impetus for renovation; adaptive use and appropriate new development in the district were necessary; and the city, in particular, had to commit to major investments in the district to make it attractive and functional.

These recommendations ultimately won the support of the steering committee, which included them in the final Downtown Area Plan announced publicly in May 1986. Although this plan contained separate elements devoted to such topics as open space, transportation, retail development and urban design, the section on historic preservation was considered one of the strongest.

The final plan described Lower Downtown as "one of the most sensitive and vulnerable districts in Downtown" and called for the area to be preserved and developed through a package of actions that stimulate more economic demand in Lower Downtown and that protect its historic character by preserving the existing buildings and promoting compatible infill development.

Some excerpts from the plan capture the flavor of the city's new vision for Lower Downtown:

> Lower Downtown is an asset to the entire city and region, the last remaining historic commercial district in the downtown core...[It] could be one of Denver's great landmarks—the not-to-be-missed place. To function in that fashion, a strong, critical mass of older buildings in the area must be preserved, restored and reactivated. The preservation of only the "best" or most historic buildings will not meet the need.

[The district's] scale and existing concentration of restaurants make it a strong candidate as Downtown's entertainment center. Of all the districts in the core, Lower Downtown is the most logical for a Downtown residential neighborhood, by virtue of its historic character, existing housing base, and proximity to the action of Downtown.

The plan specifically recommended the creation of a Lower Downtown Historic District with the following program elements:

- Mandatory review of all requests to demolish historic buildings. This requirement should "draw a reasonable balance between private property rights and the public interest in preserving the critical mass of historic character in the district." It should be the responsibility of the property owner to demonstrate the infeasibilty of renovating or reusing a historic building. Buildings to be protected would be "specified in a collaborative process involving Lower Downtown stakeholders."

- Development and enforcement of minimum design standards to ensure compatibility between new and old buildings. The design review would be conducted by a committee of design, construction and development experts. Design standards would govern such matters as windows, building facades and the use of materials on building exteriors, setbacks and roof lines. These standards would be applied at the early planning or design stages of a development project.

- Zoning code revisions to reduce density bonuses previously offered for building atriums and plazas that conflict with the district's traditional street patterns and building styles. Reduced parking requirements for restored historic buildings were also recommended.

- Public investments, civic design improvements and business promotion activities aimed at revitalizing the district. These investments helped to allay property owners' concerns over the proposed design and demolition controls.

- Removal of an intrusive viaduct that represented a major obstacle to Lower Downtown's revival.

Thus a comprehensive program for historic preservation in Lower Downtown made its way into the city's broader vision for its future with Denver's official adoption of the Downtown Area Plan in May 1986. The preservation of this historic warehouse district was no longer seen as a narrow interest of one segment of the community.

Implementation of the Plan

Stage 4 in the process of establishing the Lower Downtown district centered on preservationists' attempts to secure the city council's approval of the plan's recommendation to confer historic district status, complete with design and demolition controls, upon Lower Downtown. Preservation advocates knew this would be a tough sell, and they were right. It was during this stage that the mayor, helpful from the beginning, played a particularly strong advocacy role for historic preservation.

Special design standards, to ensure that new construction in Lower Downtown would blend in harmoniously with the existing historic structures, and special controls on demolition proposals were considered essential to the protection of the district's historic character. But not surprisingly, such standards and controls provoked a vigorous debate over whether, and how extensively, the city should regulate development.

Some argued that with the decline in downtown development, no new restrictions should be imposed on property owners. Others argued that Lower Downtown could actually help the downtown bounce back from its economic doldrums if it were protected. Some property owners protested that their property rights were being abridged and that unfair burdens were being placed on them. Some owners objected that such controls would lower property values in the district and reduce city revenues.

At one point during these debates, planning department staff suggested a willingness to be more flexible on the design standards. They were overruled by the mayor, however, who took the position that such standards were essential. During this period the mayor also inserted himself directly into the debate and met with the property owners to explain why the preservation of Lower Downtown was important to the whole city.

The arguments over the economic impacts of a historic district were among the toughest challenges faced by preservationists throughout this entire effort. Although they knew of many cases in which historic districts had enhanced property values and economic vitality, they felt frustrated by the fact that no one had organized information on the economic benefits of historic preservation in a way that could help them refute assertions that historic designation would reduce property values and act as a drag on the local economy. They thus often had to scramble for facts and support.

Of all the elements in the program, the demolition controls were by far the most controversial. A number of property owners undertook a major campaign to defeat the ordinance because of these controls. An emotional and highly charged public debate ensued. At one point the city planning director advised the mayor that the ordinance could cost him his reelection. But the mayor stuck to his strong position and, along with the preservation community, managed to persuade the city council to approve an ordinance establishing Lower Downtown as a protected historic district on March 7, 1988.

Lower Downtown Historic District Ordinance. The new ordinance provided for a range of land uses in the Lower Downtown area to ensure that buildings would not be lost simply because of rigid restrictions on the types of uses permitted. It gave special encouragement to retail uses and housing.

The ordinance established a category of "contributing buildings." These included not only landmark buildings but also buildings that added to the quality of the district even though they lacked distinction when considered individually. All contributing buildings were classified and mapped. Proposed changes to such buildings, including alterations or demolitions, were made subject to review. The ordinance also permitted contributing buildings to be treated as "donor sites" under Denver's transfer of development rights program.

The ordinance sought to make the renovation and reuse of Lower Downtown's historic buildings more economically feasible by lifting rigid restrictions on permitted land uses. Through changes in allowable floor area ratios (FARs, the ratio of a building's floor area to the area of its site), the ordinance also encouraged uses that would enliven the area, such as retail stores and housing. The base FAR allowed as a matter of right was set at 2:1. This FAR would be permitted to rise to 7.4:1 if a developer agreed to provide housing, underground parking or street-level stores to enhance pedestrian activity in the district.

This system of allowing developers to build taller and bulkier buildings in exchange for using buildings in desired ways or for providing desired public amenities is often called a "bonus" system. Denver was moving toward a greater reliance upon such a system when cities such as San Francisco and Seattle had recently rejected or were moving away from the concept.

Design Review. The ordinance created a Lower Downtown Consultation Board to oversee alterations to buildings and assess the compatibility of new development with the district's historic character. Minimum design standards were established to review all exterior alterations, additions or new construction. The standards cover such matters as windows, facade design, setbacks, rooflines, building heights and use of exterior building materials. They also require a developer to break up a large building facade that seems overwhelming to a pedestrian through such elements as window patterns, doorways, columns and street entrances.

If the city planning staff and a property owner cannot agree on whether a development proposal meets the minimum design standards, their disagreement is referred to the consultation board. This board also reviews disputes over proposed demolitions. The creation of the consultation board itself, whose composition favors property owners over preservation interests, symbolizes the tough compromises made to get the Lower Downtown ordinance passed.

The Landmark Preservation Commission is not given the initial responsibility for making design or demolition decisions. The consultation board performs that role, with appeals going to the commission.

Revolving Loan Fund. There had been support all along for a revolving loan fund to assist district property owners with renovations or property improvements. The concept finally became a reality when Debbie Ortega, a new city council member who represented Lower Downtown, actively pushed it to mollify property owner opposition to the historic district ordinance. Ortega's revolving fund proposal enabled the city to demonstrate its commitment to helping property owners while still supporting the demolition controls. With funds contributed by the city, Historic Denver, Inc., the Piton Foundation, and a $200,000 loan from the National Trust for Historic Preservation, Denver put together a $950,000 revolving loan fund. This now operates out of a special business office created for Lower Downtown by the Denver Partnership, a further demonstration of the commitment made by both the city and the partnership to this effort. The fund, which provides gap financing, emergency rehabilitation funds, interest guarantees and interim construction loans, helped counter the argument that there was no public interest in these buildings.

Demolition Controls. The ordinance allows for the outright denial (not merely the delay) of building demolition requests unless "all economically viable use of the property" is precluded. Even then, a demolition may be approved only when a replacement structure has been approved for the site. The latter feature is intended to prevent the district's replacement of historic buildings with surface parking lots—a serious problem in many American cities.

Biennial Reviews. One highly significant provision in the ordinance is a requirement that it be reviewed every two years over the six-year period following its adoption. This provision states that the city council must specifically determine every two years whether to retain or repeal the ordinance's demolition controls. The biennial review requires the city council to hold a public hearing at which Denver's planning board must document progress made in carrying out city commitments in the district. These commitments, for streetscape improvements and the like, were considered critical to property owners' support for the district. The biennial review proved necessary to placate strong property owner objections to the design standards and demolition controls. Thus, the effects of all these regulations will be closely watched for at least six years.

Conclusion

In many respects, Denver's downtown plan stands as a model for collaborative downtown planning. Well-organized, well-financed and marked by extensive involvement of all major downtown interests, it has been imitated by other American cities.

But the Denver model also illustrates the risks and challenges this kind of process places on those who represent historic preservation and other downtown interests. The numerous meetings and the intellectual debates generated challenged the resourcefulness and creativity of the participants, who had to learn how to build stronger coalitions with other interests. They had to relate Lower Downtown to larger community objectives. And they had to hone their arguments carefully.

In Denver, despite the collaborative nature of the planning process, in many respects the final outcome—a city council vote of 10–3 in support of the Lower Downtown Historic District—came down to a bare-knuckles political fight. But because the process had established a good framework for the policy debate and had raised the level of understanding of the planning concepts at stake, those involved were able to carry the fight on a higher level. The debate revolved around more substantive issues than campaign contributions and important political names.

Some property owners remain enthusiastic supporters of the historic district, some are still tentative, some still oppose it. Preservationists recognize this and are committed to monitoring earlier commitments and working to ensure that they are delivered. They are pleased that the city's chamber of commerce has chosen recently to move its offices into Lower Downtown.

Preservationists assign a lion's share of the credit for creating the Lower Downtown Historic District to Mayor Federico Pena, who, in their view, exercised strong leadership in the face of considerable political risks. As one local preservation leader put it, "It was the mayor who was the most unwavering and the strongest. The preservationists lined up behind him, while he held the no-surrender line."

References

B-7 Lower Downtown District Ordinance, City and County of Denver. 1988.

"Developers Create 'LoHo' from blighted warehouses." Carson Read, *Denver Business Journal*, November 28, 1988.

Downtown Area Plan. A Plan for the Future of Downtown Denver. Denver Partnership and Denver Planning Office, City and County of Denver, spring 1986.

"New Development and Infill Construction Design Guidelines. Lower Downtown Denver." Prepared and published by the Civic Design Team, Denver Partnership, with assistance from Downing-Leach Architects and Planners, Boulder, Colo., February 1983.

Colgate-Palmolive's clock, a familiar Jersey City landmark. (Will Cofnuk, Star Ledger)

Jersey City

Looking across the Hudson River from downtown Manhattan, many people probably have seen Jersey City, N.J., without realizing they were peering at a city of 220,000 people with one of the most impressive collections of 19th-century housing found anywhere in New Jersey. Jersey City, like many old industrial cities, is beginning to emerge from several decades of decline, but the prognosis for historic preservation in this city is guarded at best.

During the 1980s, private investment revived many of Jersey City's historic neighborhoods; waterfront redevelopment has been a different story. In recent years, development pressure along the Jersey City waterfront has been so intense the local media have begun to refer to it as the "Gold Coast." Old manufacturing plants and warehouses have been demolished to make way for new office and mixed-use developments, and skyrocketing land values make any significant preservation and reuse of structures along the waterfront unlikely.

Another key element in the historic preservation and redevelopment equation in Jersey City is the state's new growth management plan. When New Jersey published a statewide development and redevelopment plan in January 1989, one of its major goals was to steer new growth into distressed old cities such as Jersey City. The intent of the plan was to breathe new life into these cities by capitalizing on the public facilities already in place there. In proposing this strategy, the state also opened the door to inevitable conflict between those responsible for encouraging redevelopment and those concerned about preserving the distinctive character of buildings and neighborhoods.

The City

In 1838 four townships on the western shore of the Hudson River joined together to incorporate as Jersey City. Located just across the river from New York City, Jersey City flourished as a bedroom community. It benefited by its proximity to the burgeoning port of New York, and during the 19th century, Jersey City became a busy warehousing and distribution center.

The western railroads of the United States terminated in Jersey City in large railroad yards on the shore of the Hudson River. Passengers and materials were ferried across the river to New York. But by the mid-1950s, the majority of goods in this country were being transported by truck, and many of the manufacturing and warehouse operations in Jersey City moved out. The Erie and Pennsylvania railroads went bankrupt.

Local government in Jersey City has often suffered from a reputation for corruption. In the early 1970s the mayor and eight others went to jail. By that time, Jersey City consisted largely of vacated industrial sites and railroad yards, decaying brownstones and row-house neighborhoods.

During the preparation of a New Jersey state plan in the mid-1980s, this densely populated, eight-square-mile city was listed as the third most distressed city in New Jersey. Factors used to rank cities on this scale included, among others, income, unemployment, tax rates and percentage of substandard housing. At the time the rankings were developed, Jersey City had one of the lowest per-capita incomes in the state, one of the highest unemployment rates and the ninth highest tax rate out of 564 municipalities. Obviously, five decades of decline had taken a toll on the city.

Despite its "distressed" designation, there is now strong evidence that Jersey City has begun to rebound. Economic activity has become intense along the city's waterfront. New York City's World Trade Center lies a mere 2,000 yards across the Hudson River from Jersey City's shipping piers, railroad yards and industrial buildings, and a fresh crop of new high-rise towers is emerging along the waterfront.

After the railroad bankruptcies in the 1950s, the New York Port Authority took over Jersey City's tube trains, which travel under the Hudson River to Manhattan, and upgraded them to today's PATH rapid transit trains. These trains connect Jersey City by a short ride to the New York World Trade Center and 33rd Street at Penn Station. This ease of access allows Jersey City to function almost as if it were a part of Manhattan.

Jersey City has promoted private commercial investment along its six-mile waterfront by helping to assemble property, by providing tax abatements and by superceding zoning policies through the use of redevelopment plans. At the same time, the city is the beneficiary of efforts carried out mostly during the 1970s by private neighborhood groups who conducted historic surveys and worked for the designation of historic districts in the original downtown neighborhoods near the waterfront.

Status of Planning and Zoning

Jersey City adopted its last master plan in 1966. New Jersey requires an update of master plans every six years, but for many years the city had little motivation to update this particular plan because little investment was made in the city. In 1984, with interest mounting in the waterfront area, Jersey City adopted a new land-use map, but with no accompanying plan. In 1989 the city's Department of Housing and Economic Development produced an "Issues Summary" as a prelude to the city's first draft master plan in over 20 years.

The draft prepared by the housing staff deals with the usual population, land use, labor force and economic development issues, but it also includes a historic preservation element. This element articulates the need to make new high-rise development compatible with the historic neighborhoods adjacent to downtown. At this point, however, it is questionable whether the draft plan will move forward because of the new mayor's lack of commitment. Some believe the plan has been shelved altogether.

While Jersey City has had no valid comprehensive plan for a number of years, it has produced a number of urban redevelopment plans, particularly for areas along the waterfront. Once adopted, these redevelopment plans replaced other planning and zoning related to an area. At present the city has 46 different redevelopment areas covering 40 percent of the city, including the entire Hudson River waterfront. Some of these plans have been completed, many have not. In the past, no particular effort was made to coordinate redevelopment plans, and it is not clear how the city hopes to merge some 20 years' worth of separate redevelopment plans, some of which may or may not remain valid, with its new draft master plan. This coordination will be essential for the city to plan effectively for historic preservation, transportation, urban design, public access and other key concerns in areas of the city undergoing major redevelopment.

State and Local Coordination

In addition to getting its own comprehensive planning process revived, Jersey City faces the task of building new relationships at both the state and county levels. The New Jersey development and redevelopment plan published in 1989 sets forth development goals for the state. It targets particular areas for growth and others for conservation. Under this plan, the state hopes to direct considerable amounts of growth into Jersey City and older distressed cities that the plan refers to as "Tier 1" cities. Jersey City is pleased with its Tier 1 designation and hopes to benefit from the state attention and investment the plan suggests should come its way.

Jersey City's negotiations with the state will not be easy, however. The relationship with the state is complicated by the fact that the state plan calls for state and local negotiations to take place at the county level. Counties are to serve as intermediaries between the state and the municipalities. The Hudson County Planning Board, Jersey City's county planning board, has existed in name only in recent years and is having to rebuild its capacity to participate in the new state and local planning process, which the state plan calls "cross-acceptance." Cross-acceptance is the process by which the state and its counties negotiate to be sure state and local plans are in harmony. For this process to work effectively for Jersey City, the city will have to build a relationship with the county planning board and help it develop an effective voice in negotiations with the state. Although this relationship is critical to effective implementation of the state plan at the local level, it does not seem to be off to a good start.

Waterfront Redevelopment

Almost all development activity in Jersey City in recent years has been along the waterfront. New Jersey companies looking for places to expand and New York financial and service firms seeking locations for their back-office operations find the Jersey City waterfront an attractive location. Despite northern New Jersey office vacancy rates averaging more than 20 percent per year, several large, mixed-use projects have been built in Jersey City in the last few years. The rapid transit connection, lower land and operating costs, and lower taxes have all helped Jersey City compete effectively for Manhattan-based firms.

Jersey City's actions to encourage development in areas for which an infrastructure already exists are consistent with the goal for large old cities in the state's development plan. The benefits of this strategy are obvious. It promotes revitalization of some of the state's most run-down areas. It also conserves capital spending by trying to direct new development into areas that already have at least some of the public facilities needed to serve it. From a historic preservation standpoint, however, it raises a number of concerns. Old cities such as Jersey City contain the largest share of the state's historic resources. While new investment offers an alternative to demolition by neglect, it also threatens existing historic buildings and districts when the land they are on increases in value and becomes attractive for clearance and redevelopment.

During the development of the state plan, preservation groups raised this concern and argued for strong preservation components at both the state and local levels so that the state's growth strategy would not strike a death knell for the historic resources that lay in its path. The case of the Colgate-Palmolive plant on Jersey City's waterfront offers an excellent example of how the conflict between redevelopment and preservation emerges in these situations.

In 1985 the Colgate-Palmolive Company closed its 141-year-old soap and detergent manufacturing plant. The once carefully maintained industrial complex included some of the most architecturally refined 19th-century, five-story brick industrial structures in the city. The complex also included some of the earliest reinforced-concrete buildings in the country and the landmark Colgate Clock, located on the top of an eight-story building. The Colgate Clock was the largest clock in the world and was

Colgate-Palmolive Building, one of the few historic industrial structures saved near the city's waterfront. (Richard Chu, Star Ledger)

described as having greeted troop ships coming up the Hudson after the Second World War.

Today, all but one of the structures on the Colgate-Palmolive site have been demolished. The 34-acre site was considered too valuable for industrial use by the company, with an acre of waterfront property in Jersey City worth more than $2 million at today's real estate prices. Two years ago plans were announced to build a large mixed-use complex of offices, residences and retail space on the site.

For the first time in the city's history, there was a citizen counter-proposal to a redevelopment plan. Residents of the Paulus Hook Historic District, which is adjacent to the site, forwarded an alternative proposal to the city council. In this proposal, they argued for greater sensitivity to historic structures along the borders of the redevelopment area and for the inclusion of affordable housing, adequate green space and other public benefits. They were supported by the Downtown Coalition of Neighborhood Associations (a coalition of four residential historic districts), a newspaper and the city council president. Even though the redevelopment plan had been in negotiation for more than a year, the council passed a resolution supporting the concept of the neighborhood proposal and set up an ad hoc committee to meet with the developers and municipal officials to ensure community participation.

The result of this collaborative planning process was a reconfiguration of several high-rise structures proposed for the redevelopment area. The tallest buildings, now to be clustered around a rapid transit station, would be reduced in height and mass as one moves south toward the residential neighborhoods and the water. View corridors, with building setbacks and stepbacks, were created to break up the massiveness of the buildings and provide air and light. Park acreage would be obtained by allowing increased density on other parts of the site. Building materials and detailing in keeping with the surrounding buildings of the historic district would be required and the grid circulation pattern restored. The finished project would include five towers—one at 55 stories, which would make it the highest in New Jersey—a 400-slip marina and a variety of mixed uses. A 55-story corporate "signature" building would be placed at the southern end of the site, however, violating the principle of reducing the height of the buildings as they approached the residential neighborhoods.

Although the Historic Paulus Hook Association was able to influence the height and a number of design elements of the project, the group received little support from the city for its initial recommendation that the original historic buildings be retained. In the end, these were lost. After it became clear that the battle to retain these structures could not be won, the association focused primarily on new development issues and the project's compatibility with the adjacent historic neighborhood. In the cover letter to its proposal, the association stated:

> The site provides the greatest potential for enlightened development Jersey City has ever known. This takes into account the past, the present and the future, and melds them with the needs of the city as well as the community. This redevelopment project could be your legacy to the current and future residents of Downtown Jersey City, if it is done properly.

The association was most concerned about limiting the size of the buildings and improving the sensitivity of the project to its surroundings.

The approach taken by the Historic Paulus Hook Association in this case is consistent with the direction set forth in New Jersey's preliminary state plan. While supporting redevelopment, the plan also recommends that design standards and guidelines be included in local plans and ordinances as a way of preserving community scale and protecting historic districts.

While clearance and redevelopment is the dominant pattern on the Jersey City waterfront, several examples of industrial adaptive use are encouraging. Close to 2,000 dwelling units have been developed in old warehouse and commercial space along the waterfront. One project, Harborside, includes the rehabilitation of a massive rail terminal building built

Grand Street at Washington Street in the historic Paulus-Hook section of Jersey City. (Rich Kraus, Star Ledger)

in 1929. The renovation and facade replacement is extensive, but the shell of the building has been saved as part of a $900 million mixed-use project. An opportunity also remains to preserve a 20-acre warehouse district on the waterfront that includes the original warehouse of the Great Atlantic and Pacific Tea Company, a National Historic Landmark. While such an area might be a candidate for loft housing and industrial reuse in other cities, many people believe today's political and economic climate in Jersey City makes it unlikely this district will be saved.

Neighborhood Preservation

While preservation is playing a limited role in the thinking and events surrounding redevelopment of Jersey City's waterfront, it is playing a major role in the revitalization of the city's downtown neighborhoods.

In the original town plan, Paulus Hook was laid out around a central square. This historic area consists of 19th-century residential brownstone, brick and frame buildings with some scattered commercial and public buildings. The downtown neighborhoods, including the original town plan area, are located just to the west of the waterfront. During the 1970s, these neighborhoods were among the most deteriorated parts of the city.

The early and mid-1980s brought extensive revitalization to many of Jersey City's old neighborhoods. This residential revitalization boom was spurred by four factors: quick and comfortable access to New York City;

less expensive buildings than those in comparable areas in New York; the large number of attractive brownstones and row houses in the neighborhoods; and the federal investment tax credits for rehabilitation. As this process occurred, many long-term residents were displaced and less wealthy residents who stayed resented the raft of newcomers. Brownstones purchased for $10,000 some 10 years ago and now restored have increased in value to around $400,000 today. While an undertone of discord continues among some older residents, overall the city sees neighborhood revitalization as a boon to downtown's economic health and vitality.

In 1974 Jersey City passed its first historic preservation ordinance. The ordinance established a commission to review alterations to facades of buildings in historic districts and designs for new infill projects within historic districts. It did not include any standards or procedures to guide the designation and review process or powers to enforce compliance with any of the provisions. Five local historic districts were designated under this ordinance in residential areas. A few years later, using the districts as a starting point, the city contracted for a citywide comprehensive inventory of significant historic and architectural resources. This groundwork assisted owners seeking investment tax credits for certified rehabilitation of these properties.

In 1985 a New Jersey court struck down local government power to enact preservation ordinances under home rule powers. The state legislature responded to this decision by passing new legislation enabling local governments to enact historic preservation ordinances, to establish historical commissions in order to administer these ordinances and to include historic preservation elements in comprehensive plans.

In 1989 Jersey City passed a new preservation ordinance, based on the new enabling legislation. The new ordinance established procedures for designating new historic districts, reviewing building alteration and demolition requests, assessing economic hardship and handling appeals. Four of the original five districts were designated again. This time each historic district was included in the zoning code and map and became the operative zoning in these districts. This provided much greater protection for buildings within these districts than that provided under the earlier designations. The fifth local district was not included in this second round of designations because of resident fears about review requirements for alterations and demolitions within the district. This district was not located in the downtown area. As a result of heavy lobbying from a religious organization and others, the 1989 ordinance also excluded all nonprofit and tax-exempt organizations from its requirements. Preservationists view this as a weakness that may undermine the integrity of the districts in the future.

In 1989 a complete reevaluation and revision of property tax assessments in Jersey City was completed. Some people argue increases in assessments were disproportionate in historic districts. Residents of the historic districts point to similar areas in the city in which houses were assessed at half the value of those in the historic areas. They also note that the city offers tax abatements to give builders incentives to construct mixed-use, high-rise towers in areas that need new investment. Recently arrived residents in the historic neighborhoods fear that long-time residents in other neighborhoods view them as rich enough to carry the rest of the city with their property taxes. City officials do not necessarily share this perspective. In the meantime, a lawsuit has been filed to determine if the tax burden is being shared equitably.

Jersey City also has a large supply of old housing outside its historic districts. Although 3,900 homes have been lost or demolished since 1970, thousands of buildings remain. There is a tremendous need for affordable housing in Jersey City, where one-third of the city's households pay more than 30 percent of their income for rent. In the newly adopted state plan, rehabilitation of historic structures is considered a preferred way to meet affordable housing goals. Jersey City expects to exceed its share of regional affordable housing requirements (6,000 units) set by the state by almost 3,500 units. However, at this point, few of these have been built. The city's many old, deteriorated neighborhoods offer real potential to create affordable housing through rehabilitation. This provides a way to stabilize the housing stock, rebuild the infrastructure of the city and meet the needs of low- and moderate-income residents. Recognizing this, Jersey City is seeking Fair Housing Regional Contribution Agreements with other municipalities through which it would help satisfy the fair share housing requirements of these other localities as well.

Conclusion

Although Jersey City occupies a unique location within minutes of Manhattan, the direction the city is taking may suggest what lies ahead for other Tier 1 cities in the state:

- The city is strongly encouraging new commercial development along its waterfront.

- It is providing numerous development incentives and is doing all it can to minimize disincentives to new investment.

- It seeks to attract private investment and increase taxable commercial properties to the point where they fund a significant share of the city's public service costs. (This last goal has suddenly become more elusive in recent months, however, because of the general slowdown in the real estate market and the national savings and loan debacle.)

In Jersey City, the change from industrial use to large mixed-use complexes has occurred at the expense of historic industrial buildings, a loss that local officials and voters seem willing to accept in order to revive their tax base and employment picture. Under these circumstances, preservation was not seen as a public benefit, but as a deterrent to the goal of economic revitalization.

But preservationists and other critics of this approach believe the city did not present all of the available options to the public. They say that when economic development and historic preservation are pitted against each other as an either-or proposition, the voters will of course opt for economic development. Both economic development and preservation can be achieved, they argue, but various ways of combining these two community objectives are not being offered. The preservation advocates also believe that more serious consideration should be given to the impact of today's financially oriented decisions upon the quality of the city's life, environment and economic vitality in the future.

In Jersey City's historic neighborhoods, the city's approach is very different. The lack of any preservation program for the old industrial areas appears to elevate the importance of historic neighborhoods as a way to provide a link to the city's history and identity. Although some believe that the preservation of old neighborhoods has up to now come at the expense of displacing previous residents, Jersey City's large stock of old housing provides a real opportunity to combine preservation and affordable housing. Others point out that neighborhood deterioration is an infinitely greater "displacer" of long-time residents than neighborhood reinvestment. Successful economic revitalization and state assistance, combined with the city's housing resources, may make it possible to provide adequate housing for all income groups. The state plan recognizes that renewal depends not only on expanding economic opportunities, but also on making a range of housing choices available and achieving social diversity.

Jersey City's stimulus to grow has been its location and mass transit access to New York City. If the state plan process is successful in moving similar kinds of growth into other Tier 1 cities, these cities also can be expected to face the challenges major redevelopment initiatives pose for preserving affordable housing, historic buildings and community character. Preservationists in Jersey City and other Tier 1 cities will be looking at the lessons of earlier urban renewal experiences as they prepare themselves and their communities for some tough battles during the planning and implementation phases of the redevelopment process.

References

Colgate Redevelopment Plan. New Jersey Department of Housing and Economic Development, Division of Urban Research and Design, January 1989.

Historic Preservation Element to the Master Plan. City of Jersey City with historic site surveys by Joseph Brooks and Mary Dieriekx, September 1987.

"Jersey City Master Plan: An Issues Summary." A report to the Planning Board prepared by the New Jersey Department of Housing and Economic Development, Division of Urban Research and Design, June 20, 1989.

Philadelphia's mammoth City Hall with William Penn overlooking the city. The statue, 548 feet above the ground, once served as the city's informal height limit. A new development first exceeded this limit in 1984. (Robert A. Presser, Philadelphia Planning Commission)

Philadelphia

Philadelphia is a city rich in historic resources—more so perhaps than any other city in the United States. Public awareness of these resources is demonstrated annually by the crowds of visitors attracted to the Independence National Historical Park, Society Hill and other historic places. A dozen blocks to the west—along Market Street where the city's commercial core and city hall are located—recent controversies over building height limits have also brought Philadelphia national attention. The height issue comes as the city makes a transition from a manufacturing-based economy to one centered on offices, services and tourism. As William Penn's City of Brotherly Love enters a new era, it faces the issue of how best to preserve its past while positioning itself to compete in the future.

In 1988 the Philadelphia Planning Commission adopted a new plan for the Center City that reflects a decidedly pro-growth vision for the city's core. Stronger zoning controls and historic preservation tools were also called for in order to better protect historic resources in the midst of the city's growth.

Planning officials believe it unlikely that important historic structures will be demolished because of a combination of factors: strong community support for preservation; preservation tools in place or under consideration; and a "grace period" of several years before approved buildings can be constructed. Others from the preservation community, however, disagree and see the pace of implementing the plan as excessively slow. In their view, many buildings and districts remain vulnerable while the city is experiencing a major downtown building boom.

The City

Philadelphia has played a prominent role both in the history of our nation and in historic preservation as a national movement. In a description of Philadelphia, Lewis Mumford noted that the city "contains more historic buildings than a similar acreage in any other American city, largely because so much history was made there between the meeting of the First Continental Congress and the removal of the capital to New York." John Francis Marion, a Philadelphia historian, describes the area around Independence Hall as "the most historic square mile in the United States." Of course Philadelphia's historic and architecturally significant areas extend well beyond the Old City and Independence Hall.

Philadelphia is a respected long-time leader in historic preservation activity. Philadelphians point to the preservation of a Swedish residence in the 1740s as their earliest preservation project. The restoration of Independence Hall, the development of Independence National Historical Park, and the restoration of Society Hill, an urban renewal project initiated through the redevelopment authority in 1954, have resulted in the largest concentration of 18th-century buildings preserved in the United States.

Philadelphia is a planned city. Although it has gone through several subsequent important planning phases, the core of the city still follows the 17th-century grid laid out by William Penn, with Centre Square (now the site of City Hall) and four flanking squares (Rittenhouse, Washington, Franklin and Logan). As this plan evolved, several distinctive elements were added. In 1855 the city established Fairmount Park to protect the city's drinking water and to provide open recreational spaces. The park is the earliest and largest municipal park in the United States encompassing more than 8,700 acres and 150 historic buildings, including the National Historic Landmark Waterworks complex and more than 10 historic house museums. The Benjamin Franklin Parkway, leading from City Hall to the Philadelphia Museum of Art, emerged from the turn-of-the-century City Beautiful movement. It provides a landscaped boulevard lined by monumental sculpture and fountains.

Philadelphia has a residential core. Developers and preservationists can point to successful efforts in the last two decades to restore warehouses, lofts and other large buildings for housing to bring new residents to the core of the city. In addition, Philadelphia has a long tradition of people living in Center City. Although many Philadelphians followed the pattern of moving to the suburbs, many remained in the city. Old City, Society Hill, Buena Vista, Rittenhouse Square and other neighborhoods provide a rich panorama of ethnic traditions and cultures from the Mummers bands to the Italian Market, from Chinatown to Germantown, from the Afro-American Historical and Cultural Museum to the American Swedish Historical Museum and the Balch Institute of Ethnic Studies. Preservation groups see great potential for additional ethnic and minority participation in preservation programs.

Philadelphia has at least 50 National Historic Landmarks within its city limits. Some claim that this is more than any other city in the country. Center City boasts 20 National Register districts—the largest concentration of National Register districts in the downtown area of any major American city. As indicated below, however, these national districts are not necessarily designated local districts, and only the latter type of designation provides real protection against the demolition of historic buildings.

Current Preservation Tools

Established in 1955, the Philadelphia Historical Commission was the first citywide preservation agency in the United States. For 30 years, the commission advised the city's Department of Public Properties and nominated individual structures for local designation. Although some 8,000 buildings—2,800 in Center City—were designated as historic during this period, no local districts were established because the law made no provision for doing so. Another of the law's weaknesses: demolition of historic structures could only be delayed six months but not denied.

In 1984, in the wake of a demolition threat to the Lit Brothers Department Store on Market Street and several town houses in the vicinity of Rittenhouse Square, the city adopted a stronger preservation ordinance. The new law gave the historical commission direct decision-making powers and expanded its membership to include the city director of finance, the commissioner of public property, the commissioner of licenses and inspections, the chair of the Philadelphia Planning Commission, the president of the city council, as well as an architect with experience in historic preservation, a historian, an architectural historian, a licensed real estate broker and two members-at-large. Compared with most other cities, this unusual composition reflects a desire to involve a number of key agencies in the preservation process in order to better integrate preservation concerns and other city decisions.

The Philadelphia Historical Commission was authorized, as of 1985, to create local historic districts; to review building alteration requests; and to approve outright, approve with conditions or deny demolition requests for locally registered historic structures or districts. Property owners may seek exemptions from these restrictions on economic hardship grounds. In considering such exemption requests, the commission reviews financial data about the property—its purchase price, assessed value, profits and losses for the previous two years, property appraisals, possible adaptive uses and studies that the commission might request. According to commission staff, however, exemptions are rare, because it is usually possible to negotiate some form of acceptable compromise short of a building's demolition. The law also includes a provision requiring that the exterior of every designated building in a district be maintained.

Despite the enactment of this new ordinance, however, there is only one locally designated district in Philadelphia—the Diamond Street Historic District with 350 buildings located in North Philadelphia. No local districts have been designated in Center City, but work is under way on three.

Aside from the city's historical commission, a significant number of private organizations, large and small, contribute to preservation, and their support, in many instances, has resulted in much of the city's preservation successes. Among the most influential organizations is the Philadelphia Historic Preservation Corporation, which provides consulting services, manages a revolving fund, operates an architectural salvage program and administers a facade easement program with 117 easements valued at more than $500 million. The Preservation Coalition of Greater Philadelphia is a membership organization involved in lobbying, litigation and education. The coalition is currently preparing nominations for district designations in the Center City in hopes of expediting the protection of areas slated for growth. The Philadelphia Foundation for Architecture is a well-funded nonprofit organization that promotes civic design excellence. The Preservation Fund of Pennsylvania, a statewide nonprofit membership organization located in Lancaster, administers the Philadelphia Intervention Fund, which provides emergency funding for rehabilitation feasibility studies of endangered buildings.

New Plan for Center City

In 1988 the city planning commission adopted a new Center City Plan that builds on the original 17th-century Penn plan. But the image projected in the 1988 plan contrasts sharply with that portrayed by *Time* magazine in 1963, when a cover story featured urban renewal and likened cities to patients undergoing major surgery. The 1988 plan proposes a different vision, one of a now-healthy city ready again for vigorous activity. This plan is upbeat, attractive, well illustrated and very professional. It highlights the Center City's assets and strengths. At the same time it acknowledges shortcomings in city services, housing and fiscal resources.

The plan's goals are three—to enhance economic growth, to create a lively Center City environment and to protect existing neighborhoods and historic treasures. The three are seen as mutually reenforcing. The plan's optimistic vision is revealed in the following figures and growth targets.

- By the year 2000, Center City can grow by 80,000 jobs, $4 billion in new investment and more than $150 million annually in tax revenues.

- The growth target for office-based businesses and development is 65,000 more office jobs and 22 million square feet of new office space. Office-based firms engaged in the creation and exchange of information are the fastest growing segment of the regional economy.

- Visitors come to Center City for business and for pleasure. The plan projects a 100 percent increase in convention delegates to

700,000 each year and a 50 percent increase in the number of
visitors.

- Retail sales can and should increase by 30 percent or about
  $300 million a year.

Visitors to the city today cannot help but see that major construction is
taking place and that these types of growth scenarios are actually being
played out.

Contrasted with the vibrant image projected by the plan are somewhat
gloomier newspaper headlines reporting that the city is experiencing significant fiscal difficulty projected to push the city far into the red this year.
This reality is an important factor in the thinking behind the new plan.
Casual observations confirm that the budget is tight. Propped against the
wall in Planning Director Barbara Kaplan's office is a chart showing a
steady decline in the number of staff working for the planning commission
and a rising share of the department's budget coming from city sources
now that federal funds have been reduced. In the hallway opposite the
office of the historical commission is a table displaying pamphlets about
AIDS and drugs. These are pressing needs in Philadelphia, according to
Historical Commission Director Dick Tyler, who explains that he can't
expect to expand his staff beyond its current five or even fill the three vacant
positions he has because money is needed for other priorities. The essential
message in the plan, in response to these needs, is that Center City's growth
is necessary to restore the city's fiscal health.

At the present time, it is reported that the 10,000 firms in the Center
City generate 41 percent of the city's wage tax revenues, 40 percent of the
business privilege taxes and 23 percent of real estate tax revenue. Analysis
of city costs, by contrast, shows that only 12 percent of the city's local funds
are spent on Center City services. Thus, Center City expansion is seen as
necessary if needed services are to be provided to the rest of the city.

The plan also recognizes that the city must compete with the suburbs
and other cities. It must attract developers and businesses whose private
capital is necessary to achieve the vision of a robust Center City. For
instance, in taking issue with linkage fees that cities such as Boston and San
Francisco levy on downtown development to fund neighborhood and
social programs, the plan warns that Center City's economic future is not
guaranteed and that the city must compete for development and for jobs.
The fear is that if developers feel they are being forced to bear the burden
of responsibilities that have traditionally fallen on city government, they
will go elsewhere. The real link between Center City and the neighborhoods, according to the plan, is jobs. Creating jobs downtown will provide
significant employment opportunities for neighborhood residents. These
same residents will then be able to purchase and maintain decent housing
and create a demand for neighborhood shopping and other community
services.

Height and Design Issues

A furor erupted in Philadelphia in 1984 when a local developer, Willard Rouse, proposed a new building that would rise higher than the statue of William Penn atop City Hall. Until then, the statue's height of 548 feet had served informally as the city's height limit. The local debate over the Rouse project, One Liberty Place, acted as a catalyst for the Center City Plan.

By the time the plan was completed, One Liberty Place had become a reality and four other buildings exceeding the traditional height limit had gotten under way. They will permanently change the face of the Market Street West area.

In justifying its break with the previously accepted height limit, the 1988 Center City Plan focuses on the impact of buildings on the street and pedestrian level and on quality-of-life issues, rather than on height alone as a concern. The plan identifies the number of buildings that already exceed 548 feet and argues that in some places even 548 feet would be too tall as such a height would block important vistas. Instead of the old fixed limit, the plan proposes a "variable corridor" approach to preserve views of the City Hall tower from such key locations as the Ben Franklin Parkway, Interstate 95 and the Vine Street Expressway. To accomplish this, view corridor height restrictions were proposed and have since been enacted around City Hall.

Defending the new tall buildings, the plan takes the view that only a few areas—namely the Market Street spine and the 30th Street Station area—would actually allow greater height. Overlay zoning restrictions elsewhere would limit heights even where the base zoning would otherwise allow it. Tall buildings would continue to be prohibited from encroaching on areas such as Independence Hall and the town house and apartment areas south of Locust. Thus the attitude has been adopted that tall buildings themselves are not a problem, and, in any case, their proliferation and potential spread are limited.

Zoning Bonus Changes

After analyzing Philadelphia's existing zoning bonus system, the Center City Plan recommended that changes be made in it. The current system allows additional density too readily and in some instances rewards features that are actually detrimental to good city design. For instance, in the C-4 zone where the base FAR (floor area ratio--the ratio of a building's floor area to the area of its site) is 5, indicating a 10,000-square-foot site could support a 50,000-square-foot building, developers were often achieving FARs of 13 to 17. In the C-5 area with a FAR of 12, buildings with FARs of 20 to 24 are not uncommon. To achieve these FARs, developers had been allowed to choose the bonus provisions they preferred. The result is that many buildings built under the present code do not contribute to the urban fabric and livability of Center City. Unusable open spaces, poorly located arcades, sidewalks encumbered with loading docks, and garage entrances that frustrate the pedestrian and diminish the urban environment have been allowed and actually encouraged, according to the city's analysis.

The plan recommends changing the bonus system so that the features the city seeks to encourage would become mandatory. The city wants to preserve the continuity of the existing streetwall (a cohesive wall of enclosure along a street), encourage underground parking while discouraging it above ground, and require all loading docks to be enclosed. In public spaces, greater attention would be paid to building facades, signs, vending carts, outdoor cafes and decoration. In these ways the city hopes both to achieve economic growth and protect the livability and the vitality of the Center City. Historic buildings would find neighboring structures more compatible at the crucial street and facade level.

New Preservation Proposals

Preservation is termed the cornerstone of the new Center City Plan. The basic strategy of the plan is to concentrate growth in areas that are largely undeveloped or underdeveloped and, as a result, to reduce economic pressure on neighborhoods and historic buildings elsewhere. Lower densities and tighter zoning controls are to be maintained in areas with an existing residential character or a pattern of mixed neighborhood uses, such as Rittenhouse Square and other intown neighborhoods where preservation controversy has flared in the past.

To prevent the loss of important historic structures located in Center City, the plan recommends that the local designation of both individual landmarks and historic districts be accelerated. No local districts have been designated in the Center City area since Philadelphia strengthened its preservation ordinance in 1984. The plan proposes that the Philadelphia Historical Commission set a target each year for designating new properties and that properties most likely to face immediate development pressure be given top priority. [Editor's note: These local designations are extremely important if the city's historic buildings are to be protected. Many people mistakenly believe that listing properties in the National Register of Historic Places protects them. As a general rule, the real power to protect is found only in local preservation ordinances.]

Philadelphia does have a number of historic districts listed in the National Register. The plan recommends that the boundaries of these districts be expanded in order to make more buildings eligible for the federal investment tax credits allowed on the rehabilitation of historic properties. Although the usefulness of these credits was curtailed by the federal tax law of 1986, the city wants to be in a good position to take advantage of the credits in the event Congress decides to restore their usefulness. In the past, Philadelphia found rehabilitation tax credits to be an important urban revitalization tool. In fact, the city led the mid-Atlantic region in its use of the tax credits.

In addition to recommending that the city position itself for federal preservation incentives that might come about in the future, the plan emphasizes the importance of local tax incentives for preservation. It calls on the city to extend, from five to 10 years, the period during which owners of historic properties may benefit from property tax abatement. It also recommends that the city explore the possibility of providing special rehabilitation financing through tax-free bonds arranged by the Philadelphia Industrial Development Corporation.

Finally, the plan advocates the use of lot mergers and transfer of development rights (TDRs) as yet additional economic incentives for property owners to preserve historic buildings. The zoning lot merger allows two adjoining lots to be treated as one lot for development purposes, even if the lots are under different ownership. The unfulfilled development potential permitted by the local zoning code on one lot may be used on the adjoining lot as a way of preserving historic structures on the first lot.

A similar principle applies to TDRs, except that the land parcels may or may not be adjacent to one another. TDRs can be especially useful in preserving historic religious properties, which do not pay taxes and are, therefore, unable to take advantage of other preservation incentives.

Preservation Economics

In order to arrive at several of these preservation proposals, the city, supported by a Critical Issues Fund grant from the National Trust for Historic Preservation, commissioned a study, "Analysis of Historic Preservation Techniques for Center City Philadelphia,"—recommended reading for any community—which focused on five types of preservation tools, comparing an array of techniques under each heading with the city's existing tools. The broad categories were:

- Regulatory measures

- Incentives

- Disincentives

- Procedural and administrative processes

- Education programs

A critical question in the study was what combination of tools might make preservation more economically attractive than new construction? An analysis of the economic impact of a variety of preservation measures on seven actual structures led to a major finding: the federal investment tax credit (ITC) played a critical role as a financial inducement for rehabilitation. No other factor was found to be as important. The study recommended a package of local financial incentives in combination with other devices to compensate for the reduced usefulness of the ITC because of restrictions imposed on it in 1986 by federal law. According to the study, a "combination of the five-year [property] tax abatement, facade easement, tax free bond financing and TDR may all be necessary to yield a 20% return to the developer unless the price of [property] acquisition declines significantly." This finding serves notice to communities relying principally on regulatory measures to preserve historic structures. Such measures may not be sufficient without companion financial incentives. After the ITC, transfer of development rights, bonds and loan programs were found to be the most effective historic preservation incentives.

Successes and Failures to Date

Philadelphia has achieved an impressive record of preservation success as a result of the combined efforts of government leaders, preservation and civic groups, and business. Most noteworthy in recent years may be the old Lit Brothers Department Store, vacant and deteriorating for years and slated for demolition in 1985. Lit Brothers is a full city block of various 19th-century masonry commercial buildings distinguished by unusual cast-iron ornamentation on the facades. It occupies a highly visible site on Market Street East. The contrast between the boarded-up dirty structure of a few years ago and the sparkling white facade of today is dramatic. Two years after an agreement was reached to restore the property, the Mellon Bank, along with other tenants, moved offices into the upper floors of what is now known as Mellon Independence Center. Ground-level retail stores are being established as well. The building was saved through extraordinary efforts and after much controversy. The new preservation ordinance was in part sparked by the Lit Brothers controversy.

Other notable successes have included rehabilitation of the Fairmount Waterworks, spearheaded by the Junior League of Philadelphia; the Pennsylvania Academy of Fine Arts, restored for the Bicentennial; the Academy of Music; the Curtis Publishing Building; the Reliance Life Insurance Buildings; and the very popular complex of buildings that constitutes Independence National Historical Park.

Philadelphia has also experienced setbacks in efforts to retain historic buildings. No better example exists than the Gimbels Department Store, formerly located across the street from Lit Brothers and now the site of a surface parking lot. Another example is the Bulletin Building built in 1906 and demolished to make room for a new Justice Center—the construction of which has been put on hold. At the current time, a list of threatened buildings would include the Eastern State Penitentiary, vacant since 1971; the U.S. Naval Home, a National Historic Landmark; and the Reading Terminal Train Shed. Construction of the new Philadelphia Convention Center will affect the shed as well as the popular farmers market, which has been in operation since 1860. Merchants in the market fear they will

Former Lit Brothers Department Store and now Mellon Independence Center in downtown Philadelphia. Once threatened with demolition, this landmark was rehabilitated in 1985 with the assistance of the federal investment tax credit for rehabilitation.

have to close their businesses during the construction period. City officials point out that the structure is deteriorating and that without the Convention Center project, the market might be lost. In addition, preservationists have opposed the demolition of several adjoining blocks of 19th-century structures for the new construction associated with the Convention Center. The Convention Center complex, however, is a key element in the new plan for Center City with its emphasis on jobs, retailing and tourism in the Market East area.

While preservation issues have been present for years, the plan for the Center City introduces a new element that promotes both growth and preservation of the past. New tools are proposed that would improve and add to the 1955 and 1985 preservation ordinances and back these with much needed financial incentives. What can be expected?

Conclusion

Planning Director Barbara Kaplan has likened the new plan to a graduation where the occasion signifies not an end but a beginning. "The focus now shifts from the plan making to plan implementation," she notes, concluding, "Those who are interested in the plan and its role in shaping the future development of Center City must organize constituencies on behalf of the recommendations they endorse and become advocates for their implementation."

Preservation advocates support the proposed preservation tools—accelerated designation of local historic districts, extension of property tax abatement from five to 10 years, financial incentives, TDRs and lot mergers—but they worry that putting these tools in place may take time. Although Mayor Wilson Goode has expressed support for the plan and the preservation recommendations, ordinances often takes months to reach the city council and gain passage. A sign of slow progress is the mayor's approval on November 28, 1989, of the new view-corridor law—a measure designed to protect views of important landmarks and sought by the plan. A draft of a revised zoning ordinance is under review by the Center City zoning committee but has not yet reached the city council.

Even when proposals such as these do pass, the city's ability to apply the new tools still concerns preservationists. The historical commission is understaffed and has adopted what some see as a "go slow" attitude toward creating the new local historic districts recommended in the plan because this would significantly increase its work load. The commission is also seen as unnecessarily meticulous in its attitude toward documenting new districts and as too politically sensitive.

The city's fiscal situation is a key factor in many decisions. Philadelphia has been characterized as having an "embarrassment of riches" in terms of its historic resources. The irony is that the city's budget is not rich. A number of currently threatened landmarks are in public ownership, with prospects for restoration slim unless significant public support develops, as was the case with the City Hall restoration work. Continued delay in deciding the fate of these buildings may sacrifice them to economic pressure. In the short run, at least, it will be difficult to balance preservation and development when the city budget itself is not balanced. In the long run, it can be hoped that the plan's balanced vision prevails.

References

"Analysis of Preservation Techniques for Center City Philadelphia." Philadelphia City Planning Commission, John Rahenkamp Consultants, October 30, 1986.

The Plan for Center City. Philadelphia City Planning Commission, January 1986.

"Transferable Development Rights Programs." Planning Advisory Service. Report No. 401. Richard J. Roddewig and Cheryl A. Inghram. American Planning Association, Chicago, May 1987.

NOTE: *Portions of the section on Philadelphia were adapted from materials prepared by the Mid-Atlantic Regional Office of the National Trust for Historic Preservation.*

Hotel Roanoke, donated to Virginia Tech by Norfolk Southern Railroad. The building may return to use as a hotel with facilities adapted for a hotel management training program. The city of Roanoke is considering constructing a conference center to adjoin the hotel. (Heywood P. Dunlap/City of Roanoke)

Roanoke

A basic recipe for success for cities, as well as individuals, might go something like this—figure out what you want, build support for it, identify the steps to reach it and adjust when things don't work out. Ten years ago, Roanoke, Va., began applying these four ingredients as a way to pull its downtown and neighborhoods out of a severe slump and to overcome a number of competitive disadvantages—modest size, a heavy tax burden and a location 200 miles from the hot development belt that runs from the Washington, D.C., suburbs to Tidewater Virginia.

In deciding what this city of 100,000 had to offer businesses and residents—many of whom had left for the suburbs or for other parts of the state in the previous decade—Roanoke's business and government leaders came to see the area's heritage as one of its greatest assets. While much of the downtown had been cleared as part of urban renewal, there remained intact blocks of retail structures from the late 1800s and an active farmers market that had been in continuous use for 100 years. Near downtown you could find turn-of-the-century neighborhoods and a warehouse area that offered attractive space at affordable prices. City leaders also realized that the Blue Ridge Mountains, a backdrop for the city, bring thousands of tourists to the region annually, but not necessarily to the downtown. From a business standpoint, that was an opportunity lost.

From this starting point, Roanoke began to involve its citizens in an open planning process that both generated ideas about community development and built support among diverse groups. Out of this came a program that included a plan for downtown as well as a revised comprehensive city plan and zoning ordinance to protect historic buildings and community character.

Preservation planning and implementation are not easy and cities sometimes must adjust, lessons well learned by Roanoke. The city recently had to purchase four adjoining historic buildings in order to prevent their demolition and to maintain intact a viable block of structures in the heart of downtown. On the other hand, the city has taken advantage of unexpected opportunities, such as the state's decision to locate its new historic preservation field office in Roanoke and the donation of the historic Hotel Roanoke to the state university by the Norfolk and Southern Railroad. In fact, this ability to adapt and adjust to new circumstances as well as to plan may be the most important ingredient for communities seeking to revitalize their downtowns. Roanoke serves as a model of this principle.

The City

Roanoke has been a crossroads for Indians and settlers since the early history of our nation. Roanoke's river and marsh provided good hunting grounds and accommodations. In the early 18th century, the same Indian trails provided passage through the mountains for Scotch, Irish and German pioneers traveling south along the Great Wagon and Carolina roads. Settlement of what is now Roanoke began in the early 1800s, but rapid growth did not really take off until 1874 to 1882 when Roanoke became the central junction of the Shenandoah Valley Railroad and the Norfolk and Western Railroad. That precipitated a series of development "booms" in the late 1800s when industries came to Roanoke and located along the rail lines and the river. The Hotel Roanoke, one of the city's most prominent buildings, was constructed by the railroad in 1882. Wholesale Row, a group of industrial warehouses making up the city's National Register Warehouse District, was erected between 1889 and 1902 and continued operating until 1981 when the last wholesale grocer closed. The City Market National Register District in downtown hosts a historic farmers market, one of the oldest continuing markets in the country.

Residential neighborhoods, such as the three making up the Southwest Historic District, developed rapidly to meet the housing demands of workers drawn to jobs in Roanoke. Rows of turn-of-the-century vernacular structures housed blue-collar workers; American four-square homes with traditional front porches and red tin roofs housed the middle class; and elaborate Victorian mansions overlooking the river were occupied by those who could afford the choicest housing.

As early as the turn of the century, residents felt a need to direct their community's growth to preserve the quality of life in their city. Roanoke's first comprehensive plan was commissioned in 1907 by a citizens group, after it had raised money to support the planning process. Thus began a pattern of community involvement that persists today. This plan, by John Nolen, a leading planner and architect of the period, established the basic form of the city by coordinating the location of downtown buildings, establishing an orderly street system and proposing a network of parks. Continued growth necessitated a revision of the city's plan in 1928, and Nolen was again retained to develop Roanoke's new plan along with the city's first zoning ordinance.

When the third comprehensive plan was prepared in 1964, the prevailing attitude, in Roanoke as well as elsewhere, had become one favoring redevelopment over preservation. City planning chief Earl B. Reynolds, Jr., now assistant city manager, characterized that attitude as a "failure of self-directed imagination." Officials used urban renewal powers to demolish old houses, neighborhoods and a large part of downtown in order to create sites for anticipated new construction.

By the mid-1970s, Roanoke faced a problem that confronted many American cities: its downtown was deteriorating as many stores and offices left for the suburbs. In 1976 a major budget deficit resulted in a hike in real and personal property tax rates as the city tried to make up the deficit. The city's taxes on business licenses were raised to become the highest in the state. Since 1977 the tax rates have declined continually and are now comparable to those of other major cities in Virginia. From this low point, a sort of challenge and response pattern began. Fortunately for preservationists, some neighborhoods and downtown areas had survived these vicissitudes.

In 1978 a young, energetic city manager was hired by the business-backed city council. Included on that council was the current mayor, Noel C. Taylor, a well-respected, black Republican minister who has been reelected by a large margin in each election since 1976. Putting the city back on its feet became an overriding goal of the council. It was during the late 1970s and early 1980s that many saw the beginning of a turnaround in the community. City officials, business leaders and residents began to work together; such collaboration has become the hallmark of the way things are done in Roanoke.

Community Involvement

Design '79, the moniker hung on this new revitalization effort, marked the beginning of the new collaborative planning era and emphasized extensive community involvement to revitalize downtown. The purpose of this jointly sponsored city and business study was to identify ways to increase Roanoke's tax base, provide additional jobs, stabilize the existing economy, attract tourists, reuse existing buildings and generally make the downtown an attractive place for current businesses as well as new investment. In conducting the study, the city designed an open planning process that has become the prototype for projects since then.

During the five months that the study was under way, a storefront office in the downtown was staffed full time. Project work was carried out there in full view of passersby who were invited to drop in and offer suggestions. Four prime-time "Design-A-Thons" were held at the local television station and citizens were encouraged to call in for live on-air discussions with architects, planners and other team members. A series of workshops and a steering committee provided additional citizen input.

Considerable enthusiasm developed and a wide range of ideas for action emerged. Improvements to the historic farmers market and the renovation and conversion of an adjoining warehouse into a cultural center were among the projects generated by this process. The surrounding City Market Historic District containing 60 commercial buildings in its six blocks and the Roanoke Warehouse Historic District a few blocks to the north were officially designated as historic soon afterwards. According to a 1984 follow-up evaluation, most of the Design '79 actions have been successful.

In 1980 the Roanoke Neighborhood Partnership, a collaborative effort involving neighborhood as well as city leaders, repeated the city's commitment to citizen involvement. A citywide forum attracted more than 500 participants after attention was focused on neighborhood issues through newspaper ads, public service announcements and surveys distributed through grocery stores, churches and schools. Four neighborhoods were subsequently selected as revitalization targets and 400 to 500 resident volunteers participated in workshops to identify neighborhood issues and resources and to develop action plans. Neighborhood leaders were sent to national neighborhood conferences and residents from other cities around the state were brought to Roanoke to share perspectives and experiences. A neighborhood leaders council was established to meet regularly with the city manager as well as a steering committee appointed by the city council. Today the Roanoke Neighborhood Partnership maintains a professionally staffed office in city hall to provide planning, liaison and advocacy for neighborhood concerns.

This style of open planning and consensus building was again employed in 1985 in the Roanoke Vision project that resulted in sweeping changes in the city's comprehensive plan and zoning regulations guiding future development. To help the city integrate historic preservation into its plan and zoning ordinance, the National Trust for Historic Preservation assisted the Vision process through a Critical Issues Fund grant.

Roanoke Vision used techniques similar to those pioneered under Design '79. The city inserted a public opinion survey in the newspaper distributed to more than 165,000 homes. The survey gave information about the history of planning in the city, issues facing the community and the Roanoke Vision process itself; then it solicited citizen opinion on these issues. Jobs, maintaining the city as the core of the region and neighborhood conservation were found to be the issues most on the survey respondents' minds. A prime-time television documentary and call-in program followed the survey. An all-day town meeting kicked off three monthly workshops to give people an opportunity to participate directly in the plan. Through these activities, city residents were given opportunities to identify what they felt was good and bad about the city and what they felt was important to its future. Regular meetings with neighborhood and business leaders were held between workshops to keep these groups abreast of Roanoke Vision's progress and to solicit additional ideas and comments.

The result of these consistent outreach efforts was an agreed-upon goal and an enviable level of trust between community groups and city hall. According to the city's economic development director, Brian J. Wishneff, this trust pays off in many ways. One is that the city receives considerable support when it negotiates development and preservation disputes. Another is the favorable publicity the city receives when it wins national awards for its accomplishments.

Zoning and Preservation

The most important result of the Roanoke Vision process was the revamping of the 1960-era zoning ordinance that threatened to destroy the city's historic downtown neighborhoods. The problems presented by this ordinance are explained in this excerpt from "Zoning: A Process for Balancing Preservation and Change," a 1986 report prepared by the Roanoke Vision process consultant Margaret Grieve:

> Current land use regulations, including the existing ordinance, zoning district classifications and demolition procedures, have had negative impacts on these neighborhoods' conservation efforts. Examples of zoning and land use conflicts abound. Although a strong historic overlay district limiting demolition and providing design controls has protected the two downtown historic districts since 1979, neighborhood areas have remained largely unprotected.
>
> When the zoning ordinance of 1966 was enacted, new office, commercial or industrial uses were proposed for many of the city's older, intact neighborhoods. The ordinance also significantly increased the residential densities allowed in these older, architecturally rich neighborhoods and made the prevailing small lot sizes nonconforming by raising the minimum lot size. This meant that a majority of the existing lots in older areas were judged to be too small and could not be developed or redeveloped without applying for a variance to the zoning ordinance. In addition, the ordinance contained a transition zone provision which allowed encroachment of inappropriately scaled multi-family and commercial uses in established residential areas. Another problem was the broad range of uses allowed within some districts without any provisions for making potentially conflicting uses compatible through site design or other development criteria. For example, an auto body repair shop, warehouse or other light industrial, commercial or office use could be the immediate next door neighbor to a row of well-kept single family homes. No landscaping, setback or other design standards would apply to the non-residential uses in the neighborhood.

Reacting to this critical assessment, the city designed a new zoning ordinance that focused on conservation and preservation. The new code consists of 18 districts, six of which were entirely new and five of which had existed previously but were modified with preservation in mind.

Changes in residential districts included density reductions so that single-family residential neighborhoods would be preserved by discouraging incompatible alterations of existing buildings or construction of new, out-of-scale apartment buildings. Minimum lot dimensions were reduced to encourage new infill housing on the deep and narrow lots existing in old neighborhoods. In Old Southwest, one of the city's designated historic neighborhoods and the second largest historic residential district in Virginia, a new H-2 Neighborhood Preservation District was created to increase the city's ability to maintain the residential character and architectural qualities of the area and to assure that any new development would be compatible with the old. Because Virginia law does not explicitly authorize local authorities to designate "conservation districts," in which special design guidelines may be applied, unless such areas qualify as full-fledged historic districts, Roanoke had to go through an unnecessarily cumbersome process in order to subject selected neighborhoods to a more lenient form of architectural review than is normally applied in historic districts. It was necessary first to establish H-1 historic districts, which called for stricter architectural standards than was desired in this case, and then to modify the design standards so that they addressed the needs of neighborhood residents. (Other state laws do not necessitate such a cumbersome process.)

To encourage more creative and flexible development than conventional zoning normally allows, the city also created a Planned United Development (PUD) program. This allows mixed land uses, the clustering of buildings, better landscaping and the preservation of open space.

For commercial areas, a new neighborhood commercial designation was established for retail and service activities geared to the needs and scale of adjacent residential neighborhoods. Under the old rules, commercial development had no design requirements. Buildings were built without regard to their surroundings. The new ordinance set site plan standards to improve the appearance of commercial and industrial projects and to enhance their compatibility with nearby neighborhoods through landscaping and buffering.

New downtown zoning rules encouraged more downtown housing and restricted building heights in the historic farmers market area. The city's consultant concluded, "None of the changes alone [is] remarkable, yet taken together they represent a new approach to removing the regulatory impediments to preservation and revitalization in one city."

The new zoning ordinance was adopted soon after the comprehensive plan was approved, essentially as proposed and with little or no opposition. The gap that sometimes develops between planning and implementation was thus avoided. Accomplishments were put into law without the slippage, backsliding or dilution that other cities have experienced.

Preservation Economics

A series of successes does not mean that a community can relax. Roanoke learned that, even with new zoning rules, historic buildings were vulnerable to economic pressure. In September 1988 the city found it necessary to acquire four key downtown buildings in order to save them.

The owner of four Victorian commercial buildings on Roanoke's Campbell Avenue announced plans to demolish the buildings for a parking lot. He had acquired these properties and others around it over the years with the intention of building new high rises in the future. The Campbell Avenue buildings were in the heart of the downtown, one block west of the state- and National Register–listed City Market District. They had not, however, been locally designated. A public hearing had been held on a proposal to designate 16 buildings, including the four in question, but the city council and the planning commission delayed action when several property owners, including the owner of the four buildings, objected. Owners were opposed to historic designations unless financial incentives were made available to assist with renovations. Had the buildings been locally designated earlier, the city could have delayed their demolition for up to 12 months and required the owner to offer the buildings for sale for preservation purposes. Even if the structures had been designated, economic factors might still have been a major issue at the end of the 12-month period.

To buy time, the city purchased a two-month option on all four properties. After considerable discussion with the property owner, who did not initially want to sell the properties, a number of prospective purchasers were identified. They considered the buildings but concluded that the $400,000 asking price was excessive. It was almost double what they reportedly were willing to pay. Just as the option was about to expire, the city announced it had obtained a grant of $100,000 from the state in order to help secure a purchaser for the buildings. In the meantime, the current owner had obtained a demolition permit and was preparing to remove the 20,000-square-foot buildings to enlarge his parking lot. In one final effort to find a purchaser, he agreed to sell the city an additional month's option. Even with the $100,000 state grant, however, no buyers were found. Still, the city was not willing to let the buildings go. It purchased the properties itself after much deliberation.

The deal was complicated. The city bought the four buildings at the original asking price of $400,000 but traded city-owned property—a building and a parking lot—to reach that figure. The traded city property was occupied by the water, police and fire departments. Under the agreement,

Historic Campbell Avenue buildings acquired by the city of Roanoke from an owner who sought to demolish them to make way for a surface parking lot. (Heywood P. Dunlap/City of Roanoke)

these city departments were allowed to continue to occupy their current premises for up to two years. After this period, they would have to pay annual rent if the city had not moved to the Campbell Avenue structures. The buildings have been stabilized and await a complete renovation job estimated to cost $1.5 million. The complexity of this deal and the amount of money involved are clear evidence of the city's commitment to preservation.

These negotiations were widely reported in the press and brought support from many in the community. However, they also prompted debate over whether the city had paid too much. Two of the six city council members opposed the purchase for this reason, although they subsequently supported using city funds to stabilize the buildings after the city had purchased them.

From the lesson drawn here—that the city's weak hand and limited time had led to the high purchase price or risking the loss of historic buildings—the city manager proposed, and the city council adopted, a supplemental preservation strategy that today calls on the city to:

- Establish a public-private, low-interest loan and grant program for rehabilitating historic buildings using city monies to leverage private funds;

- Extend the property tax freeze from five to 10 years on renovation work in designated historic districts;

- Seek legislation increasing penalties for illegally demolishing historic structures;
- Improve review procedures and staff capability in dealing with historic buildings;
- Provide low-cost preservation design assistance and a matching grant program to hire consultants;
- Pursue a more comprehensive inventory of structures.

Roanoke's effort to get the low-interest loan program established has taken nearly a year but the results are impressive.

Characteristically this effort involved many segments of the community. A pool of $2 million from eight Roanoke Valley banks and savings and loan institutions will be offered for loans at 2 percent below the prime rate. The program, along with a matching grant program for facade improvements, is to be administered jointly by Downtown Roanoke, Inc., the Roanoke Valley Preservation Foundation and the city. Already the city reports that there are many property owners and developers interested in loans. Estimates from Downtown Roanoke, Inc., are that "for every dollar lent, building restoration programs usually bring in $20" in leveraged investment. To complement the loan program, the city has established a matching grant program for facade rehabilitation and architectural design assistance using community development block grant funds available through the U.S. Department of Housing and Urban Development. Any projects so assisted must comply with the Secretary of the Interior's Standards for Rehabilitation and accompanying guidelines.

Other tools the city would like to use are not possible under existing state law. These include transferable development rights, conservation districts for neighborhoods, parking impact fees and stronger demolition controls to strengthen the protection of historic buildings.

State Support for Local Efforts

Not a city to let opportunity slip by, Roanoke has capitalized on heightened interest in preservation at the state level and turned this to its advantage. In November 1988, the Governor's Commission to Study Historic Preservation completed an 18-month assessment of the laws and programs of the commonwealth and made extensive recommendations designed to put "Virginia back in the forefront of our nation's historic preservation efforts." The report, issued just before the opening of the 1989 session of the state legislature, provided the basis for the governor to advance a number of the recommended actions.

Several of the commission's recommendations were enacted. The state's preservation agency was returned to the status of a department reporting directly to the secretary of natural resources. Previously it had reported through the Department of Conservation where the park, recreation and soil and water conservation functions were also located. The new Department of Historic Resources received funding for 17 new positions—approximately a 50 percent increase in staff. A grant program of $500,000 for threatened historic buildings and a revolving fund also of $500,000 were established. A pilot regional office of the new department was created to work more closely with local governments and citizens on preservation issues.

For Roanoke the most significant immediate consequence of the commission's initiative was the city's success in competing with 13 other cities for the state's pilot regional office. Roanoke's proposal included free space at Buena Vista, a National Register property located in a city park. The city also organized its supporters in the region to assure the state of a receptive constituency for the new office's activities. The new regional office, with a staff of four, has been in operation for less than a year but has already had an impact. It acts as a resource for preservation groups in the area, assists local governments in the region, provides design consultation and tax act assistance to property owners and coordinates speaking engagements promoting preservation. The state's decision to place the office in Roanoke and the attendant publicity are prized locally as validation by the state of the city's preservation success.

The importance of being prepared to take advantage of opportunities when they arise, something that Roanoke has done well, applies to all levels of government. David Brown, chair of the Governor's Commission, remarked, "Four years ago, preservation had zero visibility. Four years ago preservationists began to cultivate legislators and to increase their awareness of preservation. We had a governor who was willing to give preservation priority and we were ready" to take advantage of that willingness.

Conclusion

Roanoke has the basic ingredients for success—a clear sense of direction, widespread community support, a balanced action program and a management style capable of making adjustments and seizing opportunities. It is ready. The key question is, are others ready to invest in the community and its historic buildings? Much hinges on coordinating public and private developments on the northern edge of downtown and linking these to preservation.

A key block within the historic district lies opposite the farmers market. Its buildings are largely vacant and for sale. While protected by the city's historic zoning, development in the future will depend on local financial incentives and surrounding investment. It is unlikely that the city would be able again to acquire these buildings if they were threatened with demolition.

The fate of this crucial intact block will be influenced by new development taking place in the area immediately to the north. On part of this area a developer is building a 22-story office tower to be occupied by Dominion Bankshares. Some believe that the height of this structure will overpower and destroy the atmosphere of the old farmers market, but business leaders and others think differently. In their view, the tower, along with the city's new rehabilitation loan program, will create the market conditions needed to interest private developers in restoring the threatened historic block. The chair of the city's architectural review board has expressed a similar view—that the tower will benefit the market area and the historic Hotel Roanoke—and has also praised the tower design, which picks up the details of surrounding buildings and is considered compatible.

Although the office tower was originally slated to house the Norfolk Southern Railroad's offices, the railroad recently announced plans to build its own structure of a more modest height two blocks away. The city, favoring the tower development as well as the new office building for the railroad, has gone to some lengths to accommodate both; it has closed and demolished an old viaduct, prepared the tower site and purchased additional land for a parking garage.

A block further north across the railroad tracks offers yet another development opportunity for the community. When Norfolk Southern announced its decision not to go into the proposed tower, it also announced its donation of the landmark Hotel Roanoke to Virginia Polytechnic Institute and State University. VPI intends to renovate the hotel in conjunction with a new conference center, which the city hopes to build near the hotel—possibly on a site currently occupied by the railroad's offices. These buildings, while not in the National Register, are considered historically and architecturally significant by many in the community. Future development as it relates to these buildings will no doubt challenge the city, but one hopes it will take advantage of yet another preservation opportunity.

Just outside the city along the Blue Ridge Parkway and the Roanoke River, the EXPLORE project is under way. This is a somewhat controversial multimillion dollar historic park dedicated to the explorations of Lewis and Clark and designed to attract tourists to the region and into downtown.

New developments continue to present important opportunities to a city that 10 years ago faced many disadvantages. But the question remains: can the city pull off what many would describe as a come-from-behind victory? At this point, momentum appears to be on the city's side.

The lesson that Roanoke offers other communities is the importance of fundamentals—vision, citizen support and program and management capacity. The city's success to date and its prospects for continued success serve as a model of what can be done when resources and minds are directed toward a common purpose.

References

"Roanoke Vision, Comprehensive Development Plan for Roanoke, Virginia, 1985–2005." Prepared for Roanoke City Planning Commission and Roanoke Office of Community Planning by Buckhurst Fish Hutton Katz, in association with Thomas & Means Associates and Margaret Grieve, 1985.

"Roanoke Vision, Zoning: A Process for Balancing Preservation and Change." Prepared for Roanoke City Planning Commission and Roanoke Office of Community Planning by Buckhurst Fish Hutton Katz, in association with Thomas & Means Associates and Margaret Grieve, 1986.

St. Paul's skyline with Galtier Plaza and Mears Park in the Lowertown Historic District in the foreground. After 12 years of public and private partnerships, Lowertown has been extensively transformed through $350 million of investment. About two-thirds of Lowertown's historic buildings have been rehabilitated. (George Heinrich for Lowertown Redevelopment Corporation)

St. Paul

In a 1987 national survey of 320 development professionals, St. Paul was ranked fourth among American cities for the quality of its downtown planning process. The city received a special citation for its work in historic preservation, largely because of its efforts in the Lowertown Historic District, a railroad and port district undergoing substantial rehabilitation and redevelopment. The survey noted there were certain common elements among cities that ranked high in the poll: political leadership, public-private partnerships, downtown development incentives and a high level of community awareness. The revitalization of the Lowertown Historic District reflects the presence of these qualities in St. Paul.

Although historic preservation initiatives are evident in other parts of this city—even in other parts of its downtown—Lowertown is an example of a major community initiative that includes historic preservation as an integral component, but not necessarily as the dominant value. St. Paul's designation of Lowertown as a historic district was not a reaction to a precipitous loss of landmarks or previous insensitivity to its historic resources. It was the result of community recognition of the role historic preservation can play as a catalyst for downtown revitalization. In looking at St. Paul, one is struck by the wide range of coalitions forged between preservation and other important urban concerns including energy conservation, low-income housing, neighborhood revitalization, small business development and urban design.

Lowertown represents former St. Paul Mayor George Latimer's determination to transform "throw away" cities into "recycled cities." The adaptive use of buildings in Lowertown flows from a conservation ethic as much as from an aesthetic or a historical premise. It has as much to do with creating opportunities for developing a sustainable, self-sufficient city as it has to do with creating a lively urban village to complement the central business district.

Throughout the process, the revitalization of Lowertown has been fueled by a level of public-private partnerships and cooperation rarely found in the competitive climate of downtown real estate development. This, along with the mayor's vision of renewal, gives the St. Paul story its distinctive quality.

Lowertown History

Lowertown was, at one time, the "Lower Landing" on the Mississippi River. Upriver were the Falls of St. Anthony, above which was the city of Minneapolis. St. Paul grew with its waterfront, which even today works as a source of trade, commerce and recreation. With the railroads, the city continued to grow and Lowertown became a thriving port, railroad, warehouse and distribution center for the entire upper midwest.

The enterprises that located in Lowertown expressed their commitment to the area and to its long-term future by building structures of substance and style. Many of these buildings were designed by leading architects of the day. During the period of greatest growth and development, between 1880 and 1920, James J. Hill, the "Empire Builder," worked to consolidate his enterprises in Lowertown. A single building was created to provide facilities for his railroads, banks and associated enterprises. Today it is called the First Trust Center. This 16-story Classical Revival building was the largest office structure in the Twin Cities from the time of its construction in 1916 until the 51-story IDS Center was completed in Minneapolis in 1973.

The Lowertown district includes some notable buildings in a variety of styles constructed primarily between 1880 and 1920. Architects with work represented in Lowertown include J. Walter Stevens, Charles Frost and Cass Gilbert, who was also the architect of the state capitol that rises above Lowertown. As the St. Paul Heritage Preservation Commission has explained, "Layers of history give Lowertown its unique appeal." In addition to having many fine examples of brick warehouses with ironwork and stonework, the district projects a sense of unity through the widespread use of brick and stone and from the similarities in building heights—mostly four to six stories.

Creation of the Lowertown Historic District

Typical of St. Paul's politics, the designation of Lowertown as a historic district was preceded by a long period of discussion and citizen involvement. Unlike the creation of historic districts in many other cities, the designation of Lowertown was comparatively free of conflict. The survey and documentation of the buildings in Lowertown led to the district's listing in the National Register of Historic Places in 1983. A year later, the Lowertown Historic Preservation District was created by the city.

Two factors were particularly important in creating the Lowertown Historic District. One was a timely and thorough survey of the buildings, an effort supported by the state historic preservation office. The other was the availability of the federal investment tax credit (ITC) allowed for the rehabilitation of buildings in certified historic districts. Together the survey and tax credit provided the research and incentives needed to support the designation.

St. Paul's Heritage Preservation Commission, composed of 11 members, is the agency responsible for the nomination, designation and protection of historic resources in the city. Lowertown's nomination as a historic district required that the commission review the district as a whole as well as the individual buildings within it. Once this review was completed, the proposed district nomination had to be submitted to the St. Paul Planning Commission for its comments and recommendations. The planning commission is charged with evaluating the effects of a proposed district on other elements of the city's comprehensive plan and on surrounding neighborhoods and districts. Comments were also solicited from the state historical society.

With these reviews completed, the Heritage Preservation Commission made its own recommendation to the city council, passing along the comments and recommendations of the planning commission. It is possible that conflicting opinions could be forwarded to the city council from these two bodies, but normally, as was the case with Lowertown, there is substantial agreement on the desirability of a designation.

The designation of Lowertown and of all other historic resources requires the express approval of the city council. Once a district is designated, the Heritage Preservation Commission is empowered to protect its architectural character through review and approval or denial of applications for city permits for exterior work within the district. City activities of all kinds with a potential impact on the nature or appearance of heritage preservation districts are subject to Heritage Preservation Commission review and comment, and all permits for exterior work, not just building permits, require commission review and approval.

When a demolition or an alteration of a historic building is proposed in Lowertown, the Heritage Preservation Commission must consider "the economic value or usefulness of the building as it now exists or if altered or modified in comparison with the value or usefulness of any proposed structures designated to replace the present building." In effect, the commission has the authority to review alterations and the design of any new construction within the district that may impair the architectural or historic value of buildings in the district. The commission may also recommend the use of eminent domain to preserve a historic site.

The system has not been problem free, however. In early 1990 a landmark structure located in an area recommended for inclusion in the Lowertown Historic District was demolished. Although the property owner had obtained a demolition permit from the city, the commission had not been notified. The city council has since requested a full investigation of this incident and demanded that any future demolition requests be reviewed by the commission before being approved.

One of the notable aspects of the Heritage Preservation Commission's actions in Lowertown is the manner in which it has used its legal powers to create alternative solutions, support major proposals such as skyways and approve demolitions of buildings where the new development is seen as a substantial improvement over the existing building. The influence of the mayor's office is felt in the role played by the commission as well as those of other important Lowertown actors.

Lowertown Organizational Aspects

The redevelopment of Lowertown is a result of the activism and cooperation of many different players. The Lowertown Redevelopment Corporation (LRC) is a nonprofit entity created and financed by the McKnight Foundation to help implement the plan for Lowertown. A special organized unit that manages development in the historic district, LRC is governed by a seven-member board that includes the political, business, labor, arts and banking leadership of the city. Although its basic mission was to create jobs, broaden the tax base and promote economic development, LRC decided on its own that two other functions were important to this mission. Those were the maintenance of Lowertown's historic character and the marketing of the area. LRC thus initiated design-review functions to ensure that the area's heritage was protected and that new construction would blend in well with old buildings. It assumed area marketing activities to attract investors who might otherwise hesitate to invest in an area that had languished for decades. Through its auspices and cooperation with the city and port authority, LRC has made critical contributions to the development of the 180-acre historic district.

Although the LRC has no regulatory powers, it works closely with the Heritage Preservation Commission and other public and private actors to encourage appropriately designed structures within Lowertown. The Heritage Preservation Commission, with only one staff person, needs professional advice and support. One of LRC's major contributions has been to provide design competence and advocacy in Lowertown's redevelopment. Weiming Lu, the executive director of LRC, has experience in urban design, having served in that field in both neighboring Minneapolis and in Dallas, Tex. The LRC also seeks out developers, stimulates discussions and negotiations among the parties, and where possible, orchestrates the activities of other interested entities. In these and other ways, the influence of the LRC extends beyond what its capital contributions or its legal power would seem to suggest.

One of LRC's most important partners in the redevelopment of Lowertown has been the St. Paul Department of Planning and Economic Development (PED). Created in 1977, PED constitutes an agency with a span of authority and programmatic interest that, with responsive political leadership, encourages packages of preservation, good design and redevelopment that would be much more problematic if they were in three different agencies. St. Paul's redevelopment programs (including more than $15 million in Urban Development Action grants which have generated in excess of $300 million in private investment) have often (though not always) been sensitive to historic values and concerns. The development of artists' housing discussed later in this paper probably would not have been possible without the organizational capabilities of PED.

It should be noted that the St. Paul Port Authority has also contributed substantially to the redevelopment of Lowertown. Although it is independent from city administration, the authority is closely attuned to the political leadership of the city through mayoral appointments and common priorities. Originally created to promote river and harbor commerce, the port authority has been active in downtown and Lowertown development for decades. Its financial strength, management talent and bonding capabilities have made it a major contributor to Lowertown's development.

Public-Private Partnerships

Perhaps the most distinctive feature of Lowertown's redevelopment is the extraordinary level of public-private cooperation found here. Almost all downtown revitalization efforts are characterized by public-private partnerships, but the variety of techniques and the depth of the commitment found in St. Paul make this city unusual in this regard. One explanation for St. Paul's success with public-private partnerships can be found in the strong role played by the mayor's office. The extensive role played by private foundations is also noteworthy.

The McKnight Foundation, associated with the founder of the 3M Corporation, has provided a combination of "program-related investments" (PRIs) and grants to assist in the development of Lowertown.

A PRI uses the investments of a foundation's capital to further the foundation's program-related goals, rather than using just its grants from investment income for that purpose. Sometimes called social investing, PRIs allow a foundation to use both hands, the investment and the grant-making functions, to support program objectives. Examples of PRIs elsewhere in the country include the Ford Foundation's loans to the Nature Conservancy to support the acquisition of natural areas and the foundation's purchase of preferred stock in a company that provides venture capital to minority businesses. Historic preservation can be supported by loans from PRIs to acquire and rehabilitate buildings, to make loans for maintenance or restoration, or to stimulate private investment in historic

Facade of the Butwinick Building in Lowertown. Lowertown encompasses 12 blocks of historic buildings, abandoned railroad yards and extensive river frontage. (George Heinrich for Lowertown Redevelopment Corporation)

districts. In St. Paul, the McKnight PRI invested millions of dollars in Lowertown in the form of gap financing and guaranteed loans.

The McKnight Foundation made the city's largest single commitment to an inner-city area redevelopment in its $10 million package for Lowertown. This included $9 million for program-related investments and a $1 million dollar grant for operating expenses for the Lowertown Redevelopment Corporation mentioned earlier.

Another unique contribution to St. Paul's Lowertown story is a foundation-initiated process called the Negotiated Investment Strategy (NIS). Stimulated and supported by the Kettering Foundation of Dayton, Ohio, the NIS focused attention on public and private investment possibilities in Lowertown.

The NIS is a technique designed to produce coordinated urban policy, strategy and goals for local communities. Partly designed to avoid unwanted effects from fragmented federal programs and to coordinate federal, state and local programs, it was also conceived as an opportunity to create common investment strategies that would have more impact on city problems. The NIS process includes negotiations among interested parties in order to achieve better coordination. There are five key elements in the NIS process:

1.Presence of an impartial mediator who assists the parties and guides the negotiations;

2.Negotiating teams of manageable size, capable of expanding or contracting as appropriate to the negotiations;

3.Face-to-face negotiations among the parties;

4.Written agreement that contains mutual commitments from the parties;

5.Public review and adoption of the agreement with subsequent monitoring of the commitments by the various teams.

The major parties in the St. Paul NIS process were federal government agencies represented by the Chicago Federal Council; the state, which was represented by an appropriate group of officials with program responsibilities for the urban area; and a local government team that included representatives from the private profit and nonprofit sector. Lowertown's preservation and redevelopment became a major focus of the NIS negotiations. Other projects facilitated by the negotiations were transportation investments, which were also important to Lowertown's viability, an energy park and a riverfront project.

Most observers believe the NIS was an important element in focusing attention on the Lowertown effort at all levels of government. Certainly some credit should be given to the NIS for the agreements signed by the major parties, which created additional momentum within both the public and private sectors for investment in Lowertown. In the end, Lowertown received over $5 million in commitments as a result of the NIS process.

The McKnight Foundation PRI and grants to LRC and the NIS process are only some of the most prominent examples of foundation support in Lowertown. The Dayton Foundation and numerous other foundations and private investors have been directly involved in a wide range of activities in Lowertown. The contribution these public-private joint ventures have made to the Lowertown economy is impressive.

An economic study undertaken by the LRC in 1985 demonstrated that property taxes had risen within the Lowertown district from $852,000 to nearly $4 million between 1978 and 1985. The study also estimated that jobs from "existing, under construction, committed and planned projects will jump to 7,900, from 3,600 jobs in 1978." The types of investments and developments that have occurred in Lowertown include retail space, restaurants, light industrial plants, apartments, condominiums, artists' studios and living spaces, hotels, movies and open-air markets. The following snapshots of individual projects provide a sampling of what St. Paul's public-private spirit and actions have been able to accomplish in Lowertown.

Farmer's Market. The solution of a controversy that erupted over the development of a site occupied by the turn-of-the-century farmer's market in Lowertown demonstrates the unusual level of cooperation between the public and private sectors found in this city. A developer announced plans to build a suburban-style hotel, the Granada Royale (now the Embassy Suites) on the former market site in the early 1980s. Although the proposed hotel promised to bring new tax revenue and building to the district, opposition quickly organized itself around two issues. The first was that the construction of the hotel required the destruction of a 79-year-old market of open sheds and fancy grillwork. The second was the design of the hotel, which was arguably out of harmony with the surrounding environment.

The controversy heated up when citizens filed petitions and lawsuits to have the farmer's market designated as a historic landmark. The conflict threatened to precipitate a showdown between developers and proponents of the market's retention in Lowertown. Instead, with the help of the city, a compromise was worked out that elicited concessions from both sides. It was agreed that the function, but not the original structure, of the farmer's market would be preserved at a different location. The city approved the hotel's construction, but only after the developer agreed to harmonize the hotel's design with the character of the surrounding district. The developer agreed to use darker brick and less ornate wrought-iron railings, to pay greater attention to exterior detail, to construct the hotel on the corner of the lot, rather than on its center so that the parking could be hidden behind the building, and to move the hotel to the western section of the site so that the city could have the eastern section for future development. The hotel's interior layout remained largely the developer's own design with one important exception: the developer did accept the LRC's recommendation that the restaurant be placed in the front of the building so as to be more visible to pedestrians.

It should be noted that former Mayor Latimer played an important role in this controversy by asking the LRC to help come up with this more compatible design. It is also significant that the city chose to use and apply the leverage it had with the developer as a result of its ownership of the hotel site and its financing of the hotel project through the port authority.

Artists Cooperative Housing. Another provocative example of the way in which political and social commitments are intertwined with historic preservation in Lowertown is this city's response to the "Soho Syndrome." This syndrome, named after the Soho District in New York City, is characterized by warehouse and wholesale buildings being transformed into upscale art, commercial and residential districts through private investment and public encouragement.

The "Soho Syndrome" is distinguished by a sizable artist community using space in warehouses and similar buildings for residential and studio spaces. Low rent, large flexible space, generous sunlight, and such features as double-door entryways and freight elevators encourage a combination of work and living. At a certain point, the neglected warehouses become attractive to speculators and other investors who speculate that the area is likely to become attractive. Rents begin to rise, code enforcement by the city becomes more vigilant—even aggressive—and the art community senses "impending doom." Finally, developers acquire the properties and, with the assistance of public authority, begin to evict the artist-tenants.

In Lowertown, this syndrome began when Historic Landmarks for Living, a Philadelphia firm specializing in adaptive use of historic buildings, acquired several buildings in Lowertown and began to adapt them to residential uses for an upper-income market. By December of 1984, according to one account, more than 200 artists had been evicted as a direct result of the purchases of buildings slated for renovation. But the artists' community in St. Paul organized. They formed a Collective Housing Corporation which worked closely with the city's Department of Planning and Economic Development, the LRC and a private developer to create loft housing for artists.

The key factor was the purchase of the Union Depot, an important historic landmark in Lowertown, by an owner who agreed to support the city's effort to encourage artist activities in Lowertown. At that point, the kind of negotiations which seem to characterize St. Paul got under way and a creative mix of financing developed. Financing included Department of Planning and Economic Development grants, a revenue bond, grants from the Dayton-Hudson and Bush Foundations, and loans from LRC and a neighborhood rehabilitation program. A project leader from PED was able—within the confines of a single city department—to get the cooperation necessary to put this package together. A limited partnership was created to lease the units to a cooperative owned by the artist-tenants. The result of almost two years of negotiations and planning: Lowertown Lofts, a 30-unit artist studio and housing cooperative.

Although this project will not answer the total need for artists' housing in St. Paul, it stands as a beacon in the effort to combine historic preservation and redevelopment goals with the encouragement of housing and the arts. It may not be easily duplicated in other cities that do not have the energy or persistence of the artists' community or the strong community spirit which pervades the Lowertown effort.

Today, there are an estimated 100 artist housing units in Lowertown, including the 262 Studio Building, with 20 living and working units, and Northern Warehouse, with 52 units, in addition to Lowertown Lofts.

Galtier Plaza. Galtier Plaza is the most dramatic and expensive public-private undertaking within the historic district. A $150-million, mixed-use project combining historic preservation with new construction, Galtier Plaza required a complex series of financing arrangements. This project is in the heart of the historic district. It involved the demolition of some buildings, but saved the facades of others. One historic building was completely restored and integrated into the project plans. The project includes a shopping area with more than 70 shops and a new YMCA facility. The "Y" is a big attraction to people interested in renting or purchasing condominium space in the project.

Galtier Plaza reflects the combined roles of the public and private sectors in Lowertown. LRC undertook market feasibility and design studies and helped provide a substantial loan to make certain parts of the project financially feasible. Another share of the financing was provided by the port authority which, when the project suffered a financial setback, assisted in a redevelopment proposal to complete the housing elements of the plan.

Although the original developer of Galtier Plaza failed to complete this project, a new developer took over and had better luck. Today almost all of the ground-level retail space is leased and dedicated to community services. A third floor devoted to entertainment (four cinemas and two clubs) is also fully leased. Half of the residential condominiums have been sold and 80 percent of the office space has been leased. Again, the execution of this project was characterized by a series of public-private partnerships.

The Skyway Issue

One could not consider a discussion of downtown revitalization in St. Paul complete without some attention to the skyway issue. St. Paul advertises itself as a "livable winter city," and its citizens joke that their Minnesota climate is marked by nine months of winter followed by three months of poor sledding. This winter climate is responsible for stimulating one of the most visible characteristics of downtown St. Paul: the skyways.

The skyway system consists of 42 links between buildings, including 34 skyway bridges over streets. Added to the pedestrian ways through the buildings to which it is connected, the skyway system includes miles of interlocked walkways. Although the skyways represent a reaction to the harsh Minnesota winters, they also comprise a competitive response to the suburban shopping mall and an attempt to facilitate pedestrian mobility by reducing topographical inhibitors like hills and ridges. In St. Paul, they also represent part of a comprehensive plan to rejuvenate the downtown area. Naturally, people interested in investing in the area are anxious to be part of a system that is perceived as being so successful.

St. Paul's skyway system is a public system. The miles of climate controlled passages that connect buildings across streets and alleys do make for an evolving megastructure at the second story level in the downtown area. But the system also incorporates the skyways into public corridors, public lobbies and even parks. The neighboring city of Minneapolis, which also has a skyway system, allows private development and design of these structures, rather than insisting, as St. Paul has, on a uniform, functional design.

The redevelopment of Lowertown and its conversion from a largely warehouse and wholesale district to one that incorporates housing, office spaces, restaurants and other such uses, had to address the issue of whether or not to incorporate the new uses and buildings into an expanded skyway system. In the end, the city chose to integrate Lowertown into the skyway system, although that decision still stimulates concern and discussion among citizens who live there.

Some think placing skyways through Lowertown damages its historic character, breaks up view lines, is incompatible with the historic district character and detracts from street-level life. The proponents maintain that the admitted problems are outweighed by the need to integrate the buildings and activities into the larger downtown system. The LRC has taken the position that the design challenges presented by attaching skyways to historic buildings are not much different from those posed by any new addition to a landmark.

Skyways in Lowertown provoked a major confrontation between St. Paul on the one hand, and the state historic preservation office and the National Park Service, a part of the Department of the Interior, on the other. The secretary of the interior has promulgated guidelines for certifying that rehabilitation work performed on historic buildings is compatible with their architectural integrity. A threat to withhold certification for a major renovation of a historic building because of the addition of a skyway to its facade triggered a major assessment of skyways in Lowertown.

In 1986 the city created a Skyway Task Force to evaluate the system and make recommendations. The group concluded that in spite of the Park Service's "challenge to skyways in historic districts, the task force believes that skyway bridges are the most satisfactory way to connect Lowertown to the downtown interior pedestrian circulation system."

Ultimately, the Park Service approved the building's certification, but the agency also declared that it would not approve any such skyways into the facades of historic buildings in the future. The Park Service did indicate it would allow skyways if they entered through an addition to, or on the sides of, the historic structures. This is an important policy and design issue because the skyway system is widely credited by other midwestern cities with providing vitality to the downtown. The future of historic structures in these other downtowns will be affected by such rulings.

Staff members in PED, citizens who live in Lowertown, and downtown business interests share the view that they would like to create a more active street life in downtown St. Paul. Skyways are usually seen as detracting from this goal, although, as the consensus statement of the Skyways Task Force stated, "St. Paul's 'skyway' system is an interior pedestrian circulation system tying together the downtown both vertically and horizontally. The skyway is part of a total downtown transportation system." In the end, in St. Paul at least, it appears that the skyways work too well to be limited to Lowertown. The skyways have the acceptance of much of the public, and investors in Lowertown continue to request skyways to their buildings. Certainly the skyways in St. Paul illustrate the way in which historic district, design review and federal tax credit certification stimulate discussion and raise awareness about the relationship between urban vitality and physical form.

Conclusion

St. Paul is a fine example of how historic preservation can help achieve other important city goals if it is coordinated with them. The Lowertown Historic District demonstrates how a city can achieve impressive results by focusing civic attention as well as special economic and planning activities on a section of the city. Historic preservation here has stimulated both a greater awareness of good civic design and an economic upswing.

St. Paul also underscores the value of finding creative ways to address potential conflicts between historic preservation and other community objectives. The fact that a historic district will also stimulate new development calls for local governments to address issues of compatibility between old and new buildings. This in some instances poses a dilemma. St. Paul's experience with the farmer's market, artists' housing and the skyways are good examples. St. Paul has demonstrated that through open discussion and negotiation among interested parties, conflicts can be successfully resolved. Even more significant, these controversies can actually produce creative outcomes that might not have been achievable save for the initial controversy.

Other important ingredients in St. Paul's successes include strong leadership by the mayor; the existence of an independent corporation like the LRC, which is able to bring expertise, resources and a network to achieve the city's objectives; the support of the McKnight Foundation and the psychological boost such support gave to the city; a sensitivity to urban conservation; and an areawide vision. The goal here was not merely to get individual projects built in Lowertown, but rather to see that these projects contributed to the larger vision of a lively urban village.

Finally, and perhaps more important than anything else, Lowertown will stand as a tribute to the potential of public-private partnerships. As the story clearly demonstrates, it is the ongoing willingness of all parties—government agencies, private investors, foundations—to combine talents and resources that has allowed this success story to happen.

References

Chapter 73, Legislative Code, as amended by Ordinance 17146, July 10, 1984.

"Economic Impact of the Lowertown Redevelopment Program, 1979–1985." Report by James B. McComb Associates, Lowertown Redevelopment Corporation, 1985.

General Policy Statement for the Construction of the St. Paul Skyway System. Department of Planning and Economic Development, revised March 10, 1987.

"Public Decision Making: Using the Negotiated Investment Strategy." Kettering Foundation, 1984.

"St. Paul's Skyways: A Report of the Skyway Task Force of the St. Paul Planning Commission." September 4, 1986.

Westward view of San Francisco with the San Francisco-Oakland Bay Bridge showing the city's "Manhattanization," the concern of many residents in the late 1970s and early 1980s. (Craig Buchanan/San Francisco Visitors Bureau)

San Francisco

In Curt Gentry's 1968 book, *The Last Days of the Late, Great State of California*, an earthquake splits off all of California west of the San Andreas fault. The land subsides and is smashed by a huge ocean wave.

Gentry's fictional account of this natural disaster dramatizes the special character of San Francisco:

> The rebuilding of San Francisco was delayed somewhat by aftershocks which for several months occurred at the rate of 100 to 500 a day. Although there was talk of redesigning San Francisco as a truly planned city, San Franciscans were in a hurry . . . [U]ntil the bonds for the new bridges are passed (and public sentiment seems to be running against them), ferry boats and helicopters will continue to be the chief mode of trans-bay transportation. The City continues its tradition of mixing the old and the new. The Powell Street Cable Car Line has been restored but the Board of Supervisors has also taken the revolutionary step of prohibiting the use of private motor vehicles within the city limits.

Of course, everyone who read the book knew that in April 1906 San Francisco had experienced something very much like this experience. The "instant city" that emerged within two decades of the 1906 earthquake and fire provided some historical grist for Gentry's fictional mill. That instant city is the core of the city that San Franciscans hope to protect from too much urban growth and development in the 1990s.

The City

San Francisco is a comparatively small city. It is only one-tenth the size of its Southern California rival, Los Angeles. Surrounded by water on three sides, it is clearly defined, separated by a bay from its eastern and northern suburbs.

After the 1906 disaster, San Franciscans passed over the opportunity to redesign their city because they were in a hurry to rebuild. To create new axial avenues or broad streets would have required months or years of political and legal maneuvering. The "new" San Francisco was built on the same lots and along the same streets that had existed before the fire. But while the old city layout was preserved, the new downtown buildings were another story. Unlike their Victorian predecessors, the new buildings were "light-colored, masonry-clad structures from six to 12 stories in height with rich, distinctive and eclectic designs," as noted in a 1983 proposal from San Francisco's city planning department.

The city's new architecture was the product of professionals trained at or strongly influenced by the Ecole des Beaux-Arts in Paris. Collectively, these architects designed and oversaw the construction of a successor to the Victorian city that had burned.

Compared to the architecture of many cities, San Francisco's buildings are unusually cohesive. Much of the charm of the city resulted from the application of certain design principles during the rebuilding, also noted in the planning department's 1983 proposal, "The Downtown Plan: Proposal for Citizen Review":

> Conscious efforts were made to relate buildings to both the street and adjacent buildings [through the] use of similar cornice and belt course lines and sympathetic [building] materials, scale and color. Buildings were constructed [all the way up] to the street and property lines, defining the street edge and producing a sense of enclosure.

From the Depression until 1950, no major buildings were built downtown. Starting in the 1950s, however, International Style buildings began to appear in the city's financial district and elsewhere in the downtown. Many people saw buildings of this style as boring, flat-topped boxes that were jarringly incompatible with the city's urbanity.

Between 1965 and 1983, 36 million square feet of new office space was constructed downtown. During this same period, new skyscrapers, such as the 52-story Bank of America Tower and the Transamerica Pyramid, began to pierce San Francisco's delicate skyline and to alter radically the city's character.

The city also witnessed the loss of popular historic landmarks during this period. Among these were the Alaska Commercial Building, the Fitzhugh Building and the City of Paris building. The old City of Paris building, a Beaux Arts–style structure on Union Square, was demolished in 1981. The demolition took place in spite of a four-year legal battle and a petition signed by 60,000 citizens protesting the building's destruction. The planning commission president at the time supported the demolition but described it later as one of the biggest mistakes of his tenure. The new structure built on the City of Paris site, a Nieman Marcus department store, was judged by a newspaper poll as the "ugliest building in San Francisco."

In contrast to many communities, where citizens sometimes seem to accept changes in their built environment without expressing their views, San Franciscans have shown a vigorous spirit when development proposals—public and private—have threatened the special qualities of their city. During the 1960s it was San Francisco that fired the initial shot in the "anti-freeway revolt" that swept the country. The Embarcadero and Central freeways were left unfinished in spite of a $280 million federal grant to complete them. The fact that the Embarcadero simply ends abruptly still puzzles visitors to the city who are unaware of the freeway-fighting chapter in its history.

In 1971 citizens organized the first of several development-related initiatives when they placed Proposition T on the ballot. Based on the conviction that high-rises were destroying San Francisco's skyline and altering views of the city's landscape and the bay, this proposal would have limited new buildings to six stories. Proposition T gained only 37 percent of the vote.

In 1979 another initiative, Proposition O, appeared on the ballot. This proposal would have imposed height and bulk limits on buildings in the downtown. Proposition O fused urban design and historic preservation issues with other growth concerns, such as transportation, jobs and housing. It, too, failed, but it gained 45.6 percent of the votes cast.

In 1983 the first of two Proposition Ms was placed on the ballot. This proposal would have required developers to share the financial benefits from downtown high-rise construction by contributing funds to public transit improvements, affordable housing construction and job training. The Proposition M backers generally supported the preservation of historic buildings, not only because such buildings were seen as intrinsically valuable, but also because they were smaller than the new buildings allowed under the existing zoning. But the more potent and emotional issues were traffic congestion, environmental impacts of development—for example, sun blockage and wind tunnels—public costs associated with office construction, including the displacement of small businesses and affordable housing, and social issues such as day-care facilities and job opportunities for San Francisco residents.

Although Proposition M did not pass, it lost by only 1,919 votes and sent a strong signal to the city administration that a sizable portion of the electorate wanted tougher controls on development.

Preservation Advocacy and the 1985 Downtown Plan

In 1985 San Francisco enacted the Downtown Plan, a set of policies intended to protect the city's livability and character while managing new

growth and development. This plan did not emerge from a vacuum, but
rather grew out of, and built upon, earlier work aimed at preserving the
city's distinctive character. Two major projects carried out by the Foundation for San Francisco's Architectural Heritage (Heritage), a private nonprofit organization dedicated to the preservation of architectural resources,
were later to influence the content of the Downtown Plan.

The first of these projects was a comprehensive, detailed survey and
classification of architectural landmarks in San Francisco's downtown.
Completed in 1979 and published in the form of a book, *Splendid Survivors*,
this survey established an objective basis for conferring official landmark
status upon—and thus also protection for—historic and architecturally
distinctive buildings. In 1982 the survey was expanded to all parts of the
downtown plan area.

Prepared by Michael Corbett, the Heritage survey employed an evaluation system similar to one developed by Howard Kalman in a book
published by the Canadian government in 1978 for surveys in Canadian
cities. The system calls for an independent panel of experts to evaluate and
rate individual buildings. The rating categories include architectural significance, historical significance, environmental significance and design
integrity. Each of these categories is subdivided into elements. For example, the architectural significance category is subdivided into components
of style, construction, age, architect's importance, design and interior
features. Each building can be recorded, assessed and scored according to
this system.

The system's recognition of the environmental and urban design significance of buildings and districts is worth noting. The relationship of
buildings to streets, open space, vistas and the sun are important public
concerns. When these environmental features are combined with architectural and historical qualities, they can engender broader public support for
landmark protection measures than might otherwise exist.

The evaluation system is more inclusive than that used to determine
the eligibility of buildings for the National Register of Historic Places, but
it can be used for that purpose as well.

The value of having an objective analysis of local historic resources
cannot be overstated. As Heritage noted in its introduction to the survey,
city planning officials, real estate interests and political leaders see objectivity in historic resource evaluation systems as being essential to realizing
the goals of preservation. It might be added that the courts, too, see such
objectivity as important when ruling on legal challenges to local preservation ordinances.

The second Heritage project was prompted by the release in May 1981
of a report prepared by the city planning department. This report, "Guiding Downtown Development," contained recommendations for new
downtown development policies. The recommendations were expected to
be officially adopted in some form the following year.

Because the city planning department's report had a potential impact on the human environment, California law required that it be subjected to public scrutiny through an environmental impact review (EIR) process. Recognizing the potentially far-reaching implications for historic preservation of the policies in the offing, Heritage decided to take advantage of the opportunities offered by the EIR process to try to shape these policies. In August 1981 Heritage submitted an application for a $25,000 Critical Issues Fund grant to the National Trust for Historic Preservation in the hope of obtaining funds to hire professional experts to analyze downtown preservation techniques used around the country and to assess their applicability to San Francisco. Understanding that a technically competent study could not only bolster preservation goals in San Francisco but also provide a resource of national interest for downtown conservation programs, the National Trust approved the grant.

Prepared by John M. Sanger and Associates, the study completed for Heritage in November 1982 evaluated preservation tools in 11 major cities. Entitled "A Preservation Strategy for Downtown San Francisco," the study recommended strong controls on the demolition of architecturally significant buildings, the creation of specially protected conservation districts and a transfer of development rights (TDR) program to encourage the preservation of historic buildings.

While recommending San Francisco's adoption of a TDR program as a way of making landmark preservation more financially attractive to property owners, the Sanger study cautioned that such a program would not work unless it were coupled with clear restrictions on the demolition of architecturally significant buildings:

> [T]he limited experience [that other cities have had] with TDRs does indicate that a TDR program will not operate successfully where TDRs are only provided as voluntary discretionary bonuses and their use is solely [driven by the private market]. Direct regulation of [the] demolition of significant buildings is required both as a basis for a workable transfer of development rights program and to assure their preservation.

While emphasizing the importance of coupling TDRs with strong controls on the demolition of landmarks, the study also stressed that a TDR program must deal with the realities of the real estate market:

- A transfer program must be able to operate consistently over time, with stability and predictability in terms of applicable land use regulations, price and availability of supply;

- There must be realistic incentives to buy and sell TDRs. For the seller, the prospects of potential development must be reasonably uncertain or negative; for the buyer, there must be either a requirement for purchase (of TDRs) or a strong economic incentive to increase development potential;

- TDR prices must be reasonably related to the value of donor sites and acceptable costs for new development at receiver sites;

- TDRs must be related to priorities for site protection (for example, historic site protection); and

- A market for TDRs must be created and probably must be stimulated by auctions or a TDR bank where TDRs can be bought and sold.

During the same time that Heritage was working on these projects, the city planning department was also generating policy proposals that, whether one favored them or not, were and remain remarkable for their boldness and creativity. Working under the direction of Dean Macris, the department in August 1983 released a precursor to the plan ultimately adopted two years later. Entitled "The Downtown Plan: Proposal for Citizen Review," this document not only picked up on historic preservation concepts advocated by Heritage, but it also recommended that the city mandate a variety of features—all aimed at creating an interesting, people-oriented downtown—in new development projects. These included such features as access to the sun, works of art viewable by the public, expressive and sculpted building tops, and downtown open spaces usable by the public. The planning department also repudiated building density bonuses that in the past had resulted in little more than wind-swept plazas that few people enjoyed.

In a February 1984 *Planning* magazine article, George Williams, assistant director of the planning department, characterized the spirit of these proposals:

> The downtown plan envisions a central area where almost everyone would be within 900 feet [approximately two blocks] of a publicly accessible space in which to sit, eat a brown bag lunch and people watch.

The planning department's ideas about transportation policy were also remarkable and differed greatly from those of many other cities. A draft downtown plan asserted that San Francisco's fragile environment was "too important to be dismantled and disrupted by the scale and infrastructure required to support an 'automobile first' policy." The planners advocated ridesharing, an increase in the percentage of downtown commuters using public transit from 64 to 70 percent, rapid transit lines, reductions in the automobile capacity of bridges and highways entering the city, limits on downtown parking, restrictions on auto-oriented drive-in establishments, and tearing down an entire section of the Embarcadero Freeway.

In short, the planning department advocated a "transit first," pedestrian-friendly transportation policy and took the view that "the automobile cannot serve as the primary means of travel to and from the downtown" without destroying the city. Although these policy concepts fell outside the plan's preservation chapter, they had profound implications for the future preservation of local historic resources and San Francisco's livability.

Protecting Significant Buildings Through the Downtown Plan

The efforts to protect the quality of life in San Francisco carried out by Heritage, the city planning department and others culminated on September 17, 1985, when former Mayor Dianne Feinstein signed a new and comprehensive Downtown Plan into law. "Today is a milestone in San Francisco's history," said the mayor, "and a giant step for city planning everywhere. This plan gives San Francisco clear patterns for controlling its future growth."

It is important to note that, in contrast to the plans in many local jurisdictions, the San Francisco Downtown Plan embodied zoning regulations as well. Taken as a whole, this document has the force of law.

In addition to establishing rules for commercial, residential and transportation-related development in San Francisco's central business district, the Downtown Plan devoted an entire chapter to historic preservation. The hand of Heritage could be seen throughout this chapter, which was entitled "Preserving the Past." Provisions in the plan that related to historic preservation and urban design included:

- Landmarks rating and identification system;
- Ban against the demolition or alteration of the city's 250 most important landmarks;
- Six architectural conservation districts;
- Transfer of development (TDR) rights program to make the preservation of historic and architecturally significant buildings more financially attractive;
- Financial penalties to discourage the "demolition by neglect" of historic and architectural landmarks;
- Major downzoning in the city's downtown area;
- Overall cap on new downtown office space of 2.85 million square feet over three years, or an average annual cap of 950,000 square feet; and
- Guidelines for new architecture to encourage more interesting buildings and an environment more attractive to pedestrians.

Landmark Ratings and Demolition Controls. Whether downtown historic buildings were protected from demolition or benefited by the new TDR program depended on their classification. The plan identified two

Russ Building in downtown San Francisco, now protected under the Downtown Plan. (Foundation for San Francisco's Architectural Heritage)

types of buildings in the downtown ("C-3") zoning district: significant and contributory.

Significant buildings, considered the most valuable, included structures that were at least 40 years old, important in their own right, excellent in architectural design and influential in establishing the distinctive character of an area. The plan stated that they could not be altered or demolished unless there were an "imminent safety hazard" or "no substantial remaining market value or reasonable use" available to the owner.

Contributory buildings also had to be at least 40 years old, but they were defined as being of "contextual" rather than individual importance. That is, they had to contribute positively to the character of an area, but they did not need to be exceptionally important on their own. Although the downtown plan did not ban the demolition of contributory buildings, as it did in the case of significant buildings, it did provide major economic incentives favoring their retention.

All other buildings in the downtown were considered unrated and could be altered or demolished with few restrictions.

Architectural Conservation Districts. The Downtown Plan also established six conservation districts. These are comparable to historic districts in that they are groupings of architecturally distinctive buildings, and protective measures are provided for maintaining their character. These districts are mapped, buildings are classified and protected, demolition controls are imposed and design guidelines are established for alteration and new construction.

Transfer of Development Rights. Under the TDR program incorporated into the plan, owners of both significant and contributory buildings, whether located in or outside conservation districts, are entitled to sell "transferrable development rights": the difference between the actual square footage of the building to be retained and the square footage of a new building that could be built on the "receiving" lot under the regular zoning rules. Owners could either transfer and use these development rights themselves, or they could sell them to the developer of another lot and convert the rights to cash. In a few cases even unrated buildings in conservation districts may use TDRs where the height limit in such a district is quite low to protect the street scale.

Demolition-by-neglect Controls. The plan also contained special provisions to guard against what preservationists call demolition by neglect. A problem in many cities around the country, demolition by neglect works like this: a property owner decides to ignore local regulations against the demolition or alteration of designated landmarks. The owner figures that by simply avoiding maintenance on the building, the structure will eventually become so dilapidated that it can be argued successfully to the city that the building's demolition is necessary to avoid a public safety hazard.

To guard against this type of scenario, the San Francisco plan included provisions requiring that all significant and contributory buildings be properly maintained. Failure to comply with property maintenance and building codes subjects a property owner to a $500-a-day penalty, a fee intended to deter demolition by neglect.

Downzoning. Yet another important feature of the 1985 Downtown Plan was the major downzoning that it effected. The plan reduced building bulk and height limits throughout the downtown, with limits varying according to the type of area in which a building was located. In the financial district, where high-rise development was most intense, the floor area ratio (FAR, the ratio of a building's floor area to the size of the lot on which it sits) was reduced from 14:1 to 9:1. The base FAR for the downtown retail area was lowered from 10:1 to 6:1. To encourage small, street-level retail stores, affordable housing and open spaces in the downtown, the plan permitted developers to omit space devoted to these uses from their overall FAR limits.

Allowable building heights were also lowered. The new limits ranged from a low of 50 feet in one conservation district to 550 feet in the financial center. FAR and height limits in areas where historic buildings were concentrated were substantially lowered.

Development Cap. The plan imposed an overall cap on new downtown office space of 2.85 million square feet over three years, or an average of 950,000 annually. (Owners of rehabilitated space were exempted from the cap.) The cap was not contained in the draft plan prepared by the planning department, but was added at the insistence of the Board of Supervisors. Its inclusion in the final plan reflected the popularity of Proposition M, even though this initiative had narrowly lost in November 1983.

Design Guidelines for New Buildings. Finally, the plan mandated slimmer, more interesting building tops for new buildings through revised bulk and FAR controls. (Some people referred to these as "party tops.") Explaining these rules in *Planning* magazine, Assistant Planning Director George Williams noted they "require[d] a reduction in the upper portion of taller buildings to make them appear more slender and to create more distinctive building caps than the standard 'flat-top box'....Treatments of 'distinctive building tops' could include: cornices, stepped parapets, hipped roofs, mansard roofs, stepped terraces, domes, and other forms of multifaceted sculptural tops." The plan also required that the "streetwall" of new buildings fit in with existing streetwalls. The base of a building had to include a cornice line or other feature to harmonize with the traditional city streetscape, Williams further explained.

In evaluating the overall significance of San Francisco's downtown plan as it affected historic preservation, H. Grant Dehart, a former executive director of Heritage and a key player in the downtown planning process, has observed that the downzoning effected by the plan may have been the most important aid to preservation. He notes that planning and zoning controls, by alleviating economic pressures for property owners to tear down and build anew, can often be more important to the protection of historic buildings than traditional preservation ordinances.

Proposition M, Second Time Around

Although the Downtown Plan enacted in September 1985 was seen as very advanced and even radical by many observers around the country, many San Franciscans felt that it did not go far enough. They were particularly concerned about the potential impact of proposed development projects exempted from the plan because they were already in the pipeline before the plan was approved. As it became clear that the city was about to adopt more restrictive development policies, many developers rushed to get projects approved before the new rules went into effect. Some people estimated that as much as 20 million square feet of office space could have been built (others saw this estimate as exaggerated) under the old rules because of these "pipeline" projects.

In 1986, therefore, slow-growth advocates proposed a second Proposition M to curb development even further than the plan did. This time they succeeded, and the proposition won voter approval. Officially known as the Accountable Planning Initiative, the second "Prop M" cut new downtown development by 50 percent again. It required that one-half of the 950,000 square feet permitted annually by the plan be absorbed by "pipeline" projects—projects that obtained permits after November 24, 1984, when the planning commission approved the Downtown Plan, but before the proposition's approval. Finally, the initiative made the annual cap permanent until rescinded by the voters.

The imposition of a cap on development, coupled with the application of special criteria used to evaluate new projects, led to a sort of "beauty contest" in which developers were competitively evaluated based on what they could offer the downtown. Among these criteria were architectural quality and the extent to which the projects accommodated other city planning goals. These goals included:

- Preserving neighborhood-serving retail businesses and enhancing future job and ownership opportunities for city residents in such businesses;

- Conserving existing housing and neighborhood character;

- Preserving and enhancing the city's supply of affordable housing;

- Promoting the city's public transit service and not overburdening streets or neighborhood parking;

- Maintaining a diverse economic base by protecting industrial and retail service businesses from displacement by commercial offices and providing job and business ownership opportunities for city residents in these sectors;

- Achieving the greatest possible level of preparedness in case of an earthquake;

- Preserving landmarks and historic buildings; and

- Protecting parks and open space and their access to sunlight and vistas.

It is difficult to estimate the final effects of Proposition M on the city.

The political, economic and social ramifications are still being felt and studied. A major issue for preservationists is how much the cap on office development will reduce the incentive for developers to use TDRs. It is likely the most significant buildings will continue to enjoy strong protection, but less valuable buildings may be more vulnerable. A few TDR transactions involving buildings in San Francisco's downtown and South of Market areas have been executed, but Proposition M has reduced the market for TDRs by setting a cap on the total square footage of development allowed. On the other hand, the limits on new office space may cause rents to rise, giving owners of existing buildings a higher rate of return and reducing possible claims to economic hardship.

Conclusion

The story of San Francisco's Downtown Plan underscores several major lessons.

One is that a local preservation advocacy organization can play a major role in shaping the policies that shape cities. Heritage's work on *Splendid Survivors* and the Sanger report are shining examples of the importance of authoritative, technically competent research on preservation and development issues. They illustrate the kind of planning and zoning analysis that can make a difference. The results of both projects were widely disseminated through public meetings and consultations with important constituencies, and Heritage worked closely with the city planning department to incorporate the concepts in these works into the Downtown Plan.

Another lesson from San Francisco is that citizen involvement and citizen organizing can also influence local development policies dramatically. Planning agencies and city administrations do respond when citizens speak out forcefully and organize to get their views across.

Protections for historic buildings in San Francisco were greatly strengthened by the Downtown Plan. Under the old city landmarks law enacted in 1967, an average of only 2.3 downtown buildings were being designated annually as historic. (It took 20 years to designate only 180 landmarks and five historic districts citywide.) Moreover, the protection accorded these buildings was weak: the planning commission could not deny a demolition permit, but could only delay a demolition for up to one year. Under the new Downtown Plan, 250 significant buildings, 183 contributory buildings and six conservation districts in the downtown area were designated in one fell stroke. Landmark demolition requests may now be denied outright unless the public's safety or a taking of private property is involved.

Other cities around the country will watch with interest to see what happens next in the City by the Bay. San Francisco has taken some of the most ambitious steps of any city in the country to manage downtown growth and to protect city character and livability.

Not every city is a San Francisco. Many states do not even permit the ballot box initiatives that have led the way for much of what has been accomplished here. But even acknowledging San Francisco's uniqueness, recent events here offer a storehouse of ideas likely to be useful to any city seeking ways to preserve and enhance the character and livability of its downtown.

References

Carrots and Sticks: New Zoning Downtown. Terry Jill Lassar, Urban Land Institute, 1989.

Downtown Plan. San Francisco Department of City Planning, November 29, 1984.

"The Downtown Plan: A Strategy for Preservation and Growth." H. Grant Dehart, AIA, AICP, *Heritage Newsletter*, fall 1983.

"Fine Points of the San Francisco Plan." George A. Williams, *Planning*, February 1984.

"How Preservation Will Work in San Francisco: Heritage's Study Yields a Strategy for Our City." H. Grant Dehart, AIA, AICP, *Heritage Newsletter*, fall 1982.

"A Preservation Strategy for Downtown San Francisco." John M. Sanger Associates for The Foundation for San Francisco's Architectural Heritage, November 1982.

Splendid Survivors: San Francisco's Downtown Architectural Heritage. Michael R. Corbett, Charles Hall Page and Associates, Inc., Foundation for San Francisco's Architectural Heritage, a California Living book, 1979.

Seattle's skyline with the Space Needle, a symbol of a former World's Fair, in the foreground. (James Bell)

Seattle

Most growth management programs in the United States emerged from attempts to control residential growth in suburban areas. The suburbs first confronted the fact that rapid growth, as well as economic decline, could present major problems for local governments. But burgeoning downtown office growth in Seattle, Wash., and other cities has made downtown growth management an increasingly hot topic. Ironically, this interest in managing growth comes after decades of efforts to encourage growth in older downtown areas. The Seattle story is a striking example of this reversal in all its manifestations.

In May 1989 Seattle voters adopted the CAP Initiative (Citizens' Alternative Plan), downzoning the central area of the city and putting an annual cap on the amount of allowable new office space. Citizens voted two to one for this ordinance despite the opposition of the mayor, all but two city council members and a coalition of business and labor organizations.

Most people attribute the overwhelming support for the CAP Initiative to a downtown building boom that had transformed the Seattle skyline during the 1980s. The initiative itself summarized the concerns of many Seattleites: "The rapid proliferation of large downtown office towers is creating a windy, dark, crowded and unpleasant environment in which to work and shop." The initiative blamed overdevelopment for destroying thousands of units of low-income housing, threatening the viability of architectural landmarks and historic districts, and displacing small retail businesses important to Seattle residents.

Notably, the CAP came less than five years after the city had adopted a comprehensive 1985 downtown plan generated through a broadly based, collaborative effort. Some people argued that this Downtown Land Use and Transportation Plan had not been given enough time to work. Others believe the plan's rapid replacement suggests that even broad, participatory planning often does not go far enough in addressing citizen concerns. A major concern of CAP activists was the plan's liberal vesting of development rights. Because the plan had grandfathered a number of large development projects already in the pipeline, even after its adoption, millions of square feet of space were exempted from the new regulations.

In Seattle, perhaps more than in other cities, downtown, or "everybody's neighborhood," raises growth issues encompassing everything from the quality of neighborhood life to concerns about regional sprawl. The city offers a test of how growth issues, planning processes, public regulations and incentives will affect historic preservation.

The City

Seattle is proud of its designation as one of America's most livable cities. It enjoys one of the most striking urban settings on the continent. Beyond Puget Sound lie the Olympic Peninsula and miles of snow-covered mountains. To the east are views of Mt. Rainier, Mt. Baker and other standouts in the rugged Cascade Range. The streams that flow into the sound and the ocean are the home of steelhead and salmon. These same streams—appreciated for their great natural beauty—run through land that has been logged and mined to provide an important economic base for the city.

Yet even as Seattle welcomes the "livable city" accolade and feels that it deserves the honor, a public and acrimonious debate over the city's future is taking place. The debate may simply illustrate Seattle's well-earned reputation as a city with strong civic activism and wide-open, vigorous politics.

Seattle's downtown heritage is concentrated around the lively waterfront and the neighboring transportation hubs created by the port and railroads. Since it was discovered by settlers in 1852, the city's waterfront has remained a prominent feature of the city's identity. The city's recent growth spurt occurred after many of the oldest downtown historic landmarks had received a high level of protection.

Seattle was actually formed near Pioneer Square, the city's most important and best-known historic and business district. Like San Francisco, Seattle experienced a devastating fire near the end of the 19th century. The fire of 1889 burned Pioneer Square to the ground. And like the San Francisco fire, Seattle's had some positive results: more than a million rats perished in the blaze and the rebuilding gave architect Elmer H. Fisher and others an opportunity to design many distinctive new structures, creating an architectural homogeneity that remains to this day.

Nearly anyone with a passing interest in historic preservation in the United States is aware of the efforts citizens undertook in the early 1970s to protect Seattle's historic Pioneer Square and Pike Place Market. Pioneer Square had been targeted for renewal, with 75 percent of its historic buildings slated for demolition to provide parking for new commercial and office development. But in 1970, spurred by citizen activism and private business initiative, the city created the Pioneer Square Historic District to protect the area. Today Pioneer Square is a bustling, economically productive hub. In 1971 a citizen initiative created the Pike Place Market Historical District, thus sparking the preservation and rehabilitation of the oldest, continuously operating public market in this country.

Some say Seattle's current struggles revolving around growth management are replays of the struggles of the early 1970s over historic preservation, with the same parties generally aligned in the same fashion and with many of the same arguments. But everyone admits that the economic situations today and those in the early 1970s are dramatically different.

In 1970 Seattle was experiencing a major recession. The Boeing Company had fallen into a deep slump, and unemployment ranged near 12 percent. The gallows humor included bumper stickers urging the last person out of Seattle to turn out the lights. Today, although Seattle's economy still depends heavily upon Boeing, it is much more diversified. The extent of downtown construction reflects the city's importance as a major trade center on the Pacific Rim, and as the leading financial, government and service center in the Northwest.

Seattle provides a clear example of a city that has gone from the doldrums to a booming economy. This transition has resulted in a series of growth management initiatives that deserve close inspection as a way to understand the dynamic between development and preservation in this and other cities.

The CAP Initiative

At first glance Seattle's CAP, or Initiative No. 3l, may seem foreign to other cities. Most cities do not face the kind of downtown economic growth that Seattle is experiencing, and they may have difficulty envisioning the need to limit new development. In addition, the citizens' ballot initiative—which is what CAP was—is not legally available to communities in many states. Still, what has happened in Seattle may simply represent a more extreme example of the kind of actions cities across the country are taking to protect their character and the quality of life for their citizens.

What does Seattle's CAP Initiative do? Through a change in the zoning law, it reduces the allowable bulk and height of buildings in downtown Seattle. Potential development was reduced by approximately one-third in the districts permitting the greatest heights, and by even more in some other zones. The CAP establishes a maximum height limit of 450 feet (about 38 stories) on buildings in the downtown office core and reduces the maximum height allowed in the retail zone from 240 to 85 feet (Seattle's lack of height limitations before CAP contrasts sharply to other West Coast cities including Los Angeles). The CAP places a limit of 500,000 square feet per year on new office space from 1989 through 1994 and a limit of one million square feet per year from 1995 to 1999. The CAP gives preference to office construction in buildings of up to, but not exceeding, 85,000 square feet, and it exempts projects with fewer than 50,000 square feet of office space from the annual limits.

Because developers may want to build more office space in some years than the CAP would otherwise allow, the city has adopted an annual competition for the space. This competition, nicknamed the Beauty Contest in its first round, is overseen by the director of the Department of Construction and Land Use, who is advised by a special review panel composed of the directors of the Office for Long-Range Planning, the Department of Community Development and the Engineering Department. The panel is supplemented by a representative from the Seattle Design Commission and four people appointed by the mayor and confirmed by the city council. Three of the appointed members must have expertise in architecture, urban planning, design, real estate development, commercial leasing, transportation engineering or real estate appraisal. One of the appointees must reside in Seattle's downtown.

The criteria for evaluating competing proposals for additional office space are drawn from the city's 1985 plan, which the city had intended to serve as its blueprint for the foreseeable future until the CAP initiative came along. The criteria include such things as:

- Sensitivity to context—whether a project "establishes a superior pedestrian environment and reinforces the vitality and special character of the part of downtown in which it is located,"

- Siting—whether a project "preserves downtown's historic and noteworthy buildings and/or respects the character of such nearby structures in its design,"

- Design—whether the proposed building's composition, scale, materials, color, detailing and texture make it superior in appearance and

- Environmental and transportation impacts—whether a project minimizes adverse effects on traffic, housing and the environment.

The issues raised by the CAP over the long run may well be more important than the particular height limits or design criteria. The competing perspectives presented by the CAP proponents and opponents present a vivid paradigm for downtown development conflicts.

Cited below are the basic positions for and against the CAP taken from the official voters' pamphlets distributed for the special May 1989 referendum.

The CAP proponents' position:

The speculative high-rise boom of the past decade has created a wall of sterile office towers and has doubled the amount of downtown office space. The boom has also created financial and environmental impacts, which affect every Seattleite.

Some of these impacts are obvious: traffic gridlock, high vacancies, the disappearance of small businesses and the destruction of historic buildings and low-income housing.

But the hidden impacts of Downtown over-development are just as significant.

The greatest of these hidden impacts is on the character of the city's neighborhoods. There, the pressure created by thousands of new downtown workers has helped to fuel a wave of out-of-scale apartment construction and to drive the cost of in-city housing beyond the reach of middle-class families.

The CAP will:

- Mandate that city officials study a long-term downtown growth-management plan, considering important factors such as regional transit, housing and neighborhood impacts;
- Place reasonable height and size limits on new high rises (about the size of the Federal Building);
- Keep skyscrapers out of the retail area;
- Emphasize preservation of low-income housing;
- Place a reasonable temporary limit on permits for large, new downtown office buildings.

The CAP opponents' position:

The people behind Initiative 31 think we can turn downtown on and off like a light switch.

They are half right. We can turn it off, but can we ever turn it back on?

This matters to everyone because downtown generates over 40 percent of all jobs in Seattle and one-third of all tax revenue. Since 1980, the downtown has created over 22,000 new jobs and over $25 million in new revenue for expanded police patrols, neighborhood improvements and human services for the aged and needy.

The CAP will:

- Cut the growth of public revenue for schools, police and city services;
- Raise taxes on consumers and homeowners to make up for lost revenue, and subsidize development in outlying areas;

- Slash incentives that support downtown day care, low-income housing and historic preservation;

- Spawn lawsuits that could cost the city government hundreds of thousands of dollars and put the courts in charge of planning our community's future.

Additionally, leading regional planners and economists believe that by choking downtown development, Initiative 31 will only spread office development into the suburbs and:

- Speed up urban sprawl and threaten remaining farmlands, forests and our quality of life;

- Send job opportunities for our children out of Seattle and into suburban office centers;

- Make light rail transit unworkable and clog our highways with even more suburban commuters.

The proponents and opponents of the CAP disagree on exactly what the voters' overwhelming support for the initiative means. One opponent, the Downtown Seattle Association (DSA), sees the vote as an expression of understandable frustration with the inconveniences and dislocations surrounding an unprecedented amount of downtown construction. The association admits that Seattle looked like a war zone; there were excavations, cranes, blocked sidewalks and boarded streets. With hindsight, members of the DSA concede that the city probably should have coordinated the schedules of the many public and private projects under construction, including interstate highway ramps, the city's underground transit system, the Washington State Convention and Trade Center and the Westlake retail office development. They maintain that too much construction occurred at one time, but argue that once the construction subsides, the public will be happier and better served; it is the price of progress.

CAP opponents also assert that the voters did not realize how much of the development they were fighting was the result of a backlog in the pipeline resulting from pre-1985 zoning. Supporters of the 1985 plan and rezoning argued that the new rules were just beginning to apply, and voters did not understand how much the new plan really could change development.

The DSA urged voters not to support CAP and to support the 1985 plan. They argued that it "took this community over four years to carefully assemble the new Downtown Land Use and Transportation Plan (LUTP). This plan took tens of thousands of hours of professional and volunteer time to craft a precisely balanced set of compromises between citizens, government officials and members of the business community." Former Mayor Charles Royer offered an alternative to the CAP, but it came too late to stop the initiative from being placed on the ballot. The mayor also appointed a special Advisory Forum on Balanced Growth, which reported that the CAP would cripple Seattle's growth and encourage sprawl in King County.

As the CAP voters pamphlet indicates, proponents of the initiative believe the vote represented a widespread and deep dissatisfaction with the plan. It must be remembered that this plan was developed under generally accepted collaborative planning approaches and was endorsed by the major downtown interests and the city government. Like San Francisco's Proposition M, which capped office growth there, Seattle's CAP represents public dissatisfaction with at least certain aspects of the planning process and planning outcomes. Perhaps the negotiated or collaborative planning process that produced Seattle's plan was somehow not truly representative of the full range of interests and concerns in downtown planning. It suggests the possibility that similar unhappiness may exist in other cities, even though they may not have such outlets for popular discontent as ballot box initiatives.

Seattle's Incentive Zoning Program

The CAP initiative is not the only change taking place in Seattle's growth management posture and programs. Substantial changes in the city's bonus zoning program were also made as a result of dissatisfaction with the plan.

Since New York adopted an incentive zoning system in 1961, many cities, including Seattle, have used incentive zoning as a way to accommodate growth while obtaining desired public amenities and benefits. Incentive zoning is commonly known as the "bonus" system because it offers developers an opportunity to build larger buildings through increased FARs (floor area ratio—the ratio of a building's floor area to the area of its site) than would be allowed as a matter of right by the basic zoning code. Because developers can make higher profits as a result of the additional building height permitted by incentive zoning—it enables them to sell or lease more space—they are often willing to provide certain benefits desired by the city.

The range of public benefits sought in a bonus system can extend from wider sidewalks to public museums, from the provision of retail space to employment brokerage and from public art to transit connections. The Seattle system includes nearly 30 potential bonuses including all those mentioned above except for employment brokerage.

The primary symbol of the new bonus system is the Washington Mutual Tower, a building located at 1201 Third Avenue. This 55-story building soars 675 feet above the city, more than half of those stories gained through the bonus system. It contains nearly one million square feet of leasable space. The public benefits received for those bonuses include a sculpted rooftop, a "hill-climb assist" to help people negotiate Seattle's steep hills, space for a child-care facility, retail space, a lounge area and an outdoor seating area and plaza. But the most important of the bonuses in a political and economic sense was a contribution of $2.5 million to a downtown housing fund.

Commentators disagree on exactly how many housing units this produced and on who could afford them. Estimates range from 275 to fewer than 80. Others argue about the value of the public benefits. Peter Steinbrueck, a Seattle building designer whose father led the battle to save Pike Place Market, estimates that for the two floors of office space gained for "shaping the top of the building into a chic pyramid" the developer obtained an estimated $1 million per year in additional lease income.

Although former Seattle Mayor Charles Royer has praised the bonus system—"we have built . . . a social policy . . . the hill-climbs, the day-care centers, the things that are adding a whole human dimension to buildings"—the program is under attack and was a major target of the CAP.

Other cities contemplating bonus systems might consider the negative experiences that both Seattle and San Francisco have had with bonuses. Those cities have moved to eliminate bonuses altogether or to reduce the amount of development permitted as a matter of right, to select and review the bonuses more carefully and to obtain significantly greater public benefits.

In addition to its bonus zoning system, Seattle also has a transfer of development rights (TDR) program to offer incentives for preserving historic properties and downtown housing. Under a TDR program, development rights on a site that the city wants to preserve (the "donor" or "sending" site) may be sold and transferred to another site (the "receiving" site). The goal is to make it financially more attractive for a property owner to preserve a desired building on the sending site. Although TDRs differ from other bonus provisions in that they involve the conservation of resources rather than the provision of new public amenities associated with a building development, by allowing greater height and density at the receiving site, they often arouse opposition on the part of citizens on the receiving end.

Although Seattle's TDR program was established in part to facilitate historic preservation, it has never been used for that purpose. Before the city cut back on bonuses through the CAP, so many bonuses were available that they undercut any incentive developers might have had to use TDRs for preservation. With the CAP, the value of development rights has been reduced, thus creating a new disincentive to the use of TDRs.

Seattle has also tried to use "linkage" programs requiring developers to provide off-site services or other benefits that are linked to the development of their projects. The most prominent type of "linkage" provision is for low- or moderate-income housing. Many Seattleites believe that the displacement of people and the loss of housing are directly related to downtown development and this is a serious political issue. At the same time courts have looked critically at linkage. In *San Telmo Associates* v. *City of Seattle*, the Washington State Supreme Court ruled in 1987 that Seattle's policy of requiring developers who demolished downtown housing to replace it somewhere else in the city amounted to a tax that the city had no authority to levy.

The implications of Seattle's two major growth management initiatives—the CAP and the bonus system—on historic preservation are not yet entirely clear. No bonus allowed under Seattle's ordinances can be employed if the proposed development destroys a landmark building. Obviously, this is a significant protection for existing landmark buildings in downtown. But undesignated buildings of landmark quality are not subject to this limitation. The effect of the CAP on downtown buildings that are of significant value is uncertain. TDRs are obviously of less value to owners of historic buildings if receiving sites cannot be developed as intensively. With a greatly reduced market for TDRs, property owners who might employ TDRs in preference to demolishing a building are unlikely to do so.

Designation of Historic Landmarks

In addition to its downtown growth management programs, Seattle has a special ordinance designed to protect historic sites and areas.

Under the Seattle Landmarks Preservation Ordinance, any citizen may nominate a property for landmark designation. The authority to approve or reject a nomination is vested in an 11-member Landmarks Preservation Board. If the board approves a nomination, the nominated property receives immediate protection from harmful alterations or demolitions. No changes may be made to the property at this point without a certificate of approval issued by the board.

An approved nomination is scheduled for consideration as an actual landmark designation by the board within 30 to 45 days. Although many cities reserve to the city council the right to approve historic landmark designations, Seattle delegates this authority to the landmarks board, which applies six criteria in designating landmarks. These relate to the historical, architectural or visual qualities of a property. The criteria do not include economic questions raised by property owners. Although it is critically important for a preservation ordinance to have a mechanism for considering possible cases of economic hardship, most preservation experts believe that economic considerations should be reviewed at a later stage in the process. The landmark designations themselves should be based upon the actual merit of a property.

The act of landmark designation triggers negotiations between the property owner and the board staff over controls and incentives necessary and appropriate to preserve the property. Controls place restrictions on alterations to the landmark. Incentives include a number of economic

Music Hall Theater in Seattle, also called the Emerald Palace. The owner wants to demolish this landmark but has met with resistance from the city landmarks board. As a result, a court remedy is sought. (Thomas Sweeney)

inducements—e.g., building and zoning code relief, property tax abatement and transfer of development rights—that may help to preserve the landmark.

If the city and property owner fail to reach a "controls and incentives agreement," the matter may be referred to a hearing examiner who reviews the case. Either party may appeal an examiner's decision to the city council. The ultimate authority to approve a controls and incentives agreement resides with the city council.

The Seattle ordinance also provides that controls associated with a landmark designation shall not deprive any owner of a landmark of a "reasonable economic use" of his property.

Seattle has used this system to designate close to 200 individual landmarks. It should be pointed out that, although Seattle vests the authority to approve landmark designations in the landmarks board rather than in the city council, a designation lacking a council-approved controls and incentives agreement also fails to provide a landmark with permanent protection. In other words, unless such an agreement is in place, the mere designation lacks the authority to stop harmful alterations or a demolition by a property owner.

This arrangement has led to a standoff of sorts between the landmarks board and property owners in the past. A landmark quality building may not be given official landmark status because the board believes that a property owner will refuse to negotiate a controls and incentives agreement. If designation occurs and the owner then protests any restrictions on his perceived right to alter the building, this would trigger an appeal to the hearing examiner. Any ruling by the hearing examiner could still be appealed to the city council. The effective outcome of this arrangement is to give the city council the final say on a controversial designation. A standoff exists because the landmarks board is reluctant to take action that might lead to this outcome.

Seattle has applied this general process to three of its smaller historic districts—the Ft. Lawton Landmark District, the Columbia City Landmark District and the Harvard-Belmont Landmark District. However, the latter two districts have their own community-based boards.

Separate preservation ordinances, each with its own rules and board, apply to four other districts, including the Pike Place Market and Pioneer Square historic districts.

Organization for Historic Preservation in Seattle

In addition to its landmark ordinance, Seattle offers an opportunity to consider a major issue that confronts historic preservationists everywhere as the importance of historic preservation in the total planning and zoning process grows. The organizational arrangements that might have served adequately when historic preservation programs were a small and relatively isolated portion of city programs need reevaluation as the role of preservation changes.

Seattle is a good city in which to evaluate the organizational placement of official historic preservation functions for a number of reasons. It has been a leader in creating historic districts, employing incentives to protect historic buildings and developing separate historic district review boards. It is also one of the few cities with an Office of Urban Conservation as well as a publicly chartered preservation and development corporation. The range of entities involved in preservation adds to the challenge of coordinating preservation activities in Seattle.

Seattle's Landmarks Preservation Board is organized and staffed in a typical fashion. A citizen board, supported by staff from the city's Office of Urban Conservation, is responsible for the nomination and designation of historic landmarks and historic districts. The board also reviews applications for landmark alterations or demolitions for appropriateness. If a decision of the board is challenged by a citizen, the city's process will provide a hearing officer who will review the case and issue a decision. This system offers a semijudicial hearing process to deal with all controversial issues, including an owner's right to a reasonable economic return on any affected landmark property.

Seattle has a number of landmark districts, each with its own ordinance, power and responsibilities. This produces a diversity of legal and organizational arrangements. The Ballard Avenue Landmark District has the authority to issue certificates of approval; the Columbia City Landmark District has an application review committee that makes recommendations to the Landmarks Preservation Board on certificates. The Harvard-Belmont District has a district board that includes members of the citywide Landmarks Preservation Board and recommends decisions to this board.

One of the most distinctive of Seattle's historic districts is the seven-acre Pike Place Market. The major cultural value of the market rests more on its historic functions and location than on its aesthetic qualities or building type. It is governed by a 12-member citizen board that determines the types of uses and ownership permitted in the district. There is also a Pike Place Market Historical Commission responsible for design-review decisions.

The Pioneer Square area is both a historic district and a special review district. Yet neither the Pioneer Square Preservation Board nor the city's landmarks board has the authority to issue certificates of approval for proposed alterations or demolitions. That power rests rather with the Department of Community Development acting under the general direction of the mayor.

The Office of Urban Conservation, the city's historic preservation arm, provides staffing to the landmarks commission. But the Office of Urban Conservation is a component of the Department of Community Development, which is primarily concerned with economic and physical development, not with conservation. At times this makes the office somewhat less effective than it might otherwise be. Zoning and building approvals come from the Department of Construction and Land Use. Seattle does not have the usual planning department, but rather an Office for Long-Range Planning, which reports to the mayor and works on urban planning strategies of all kinds. This particular structure poses certain challenges to an integrated downtown planning and preservation program.

Still another significant actor in the management of historic preservation in Seattle is Historic Seattle, an unusual hybrid with the formal title of Historic Seattle Preservation and Development Authority. Historic Seattle is authorized under state law to operate as a separate public corporation, but its effective powers and responsibilities are based on the city's financial and organizational backing. It is governed by a 12-member council, four of whom are appointed by the mayor, and can own and sell real estate, rehabilitate buildings and also undertake other functions, such as developing tenants and uses for historic buildings.

Recently, Historic Seattle has been underused by the city and has received too few city funds to support itself adequately. Consequently, it has maintained itself by providing technical preservation services on a fee basis and from development fees and leases on buildings it manages. In the opinion of some observers, this promising organization has been held back by opposition to its potential as a historic preservation advocate and agent.

Certainly Seattle is not the only city where the relationships between historic preservation districts and the central city landmark agency have become an issue. Neither is it the only city where the relationships among the agencies of city government that affect historic properties and districts become increasingly important to success. Seattle does serve to illustrate the issues that arise as strong programs and engaged citizens achieve success. It is not farfetched to suggest that organizational skills and relationships will become as important to historic preservation success as formal legal authority.

Conclusion

The story in Seattle is not over. There will be efforts to repeal the CAP, which the law allows after a two-year period. If that is undertaken, a more far-ranging review of growth management issues will face Seattle's downtown. If that happens, neighborhood concerns and the regional growth patterns will also have to be addressed.

As we have noted, Seattle moves the issue of city organization for planning and historic preservation into the forefront of concerns. Some observers believe that the system works well through heroic efforts of coordination and good will. Yet the passage of the CAP initiative indicates what some call a significant undercurrent of discontent with the city's overall success in preserving its downtown.

Concern about the rate and type of growth in downtown Seattle has set a number of things in motion. The cap on new downtown office space, the revisions of the bonus zoning program and the attempt to link preservation with overall planning efforts are likely to be watched closely by other cities as they take steps to improve and protect the livability of their downtowns.

References

Land Use and Transportation Plan for Downtown Seattle, City of Seattle. Adopted June 10, 1985, by Resolution 27281, November 1985.

1989 Voters Pamphlet, Initiative Measure No. 31, to the People Special Election. Tuesday, May 16, 1989. Office of Election Administration, City of Seattle.

Seattle's Role in Regional Growth: Final Report—The Advisory Forum on Balanced Growth. February 1989.

"Historic Preservation in Seattle: A Guide to Incentives and Procedures." Department of Community Development, City of Seattle, August 1988.

Director's Rule 11:85, Public Benefit Features: Guidelines for Evaluating Projects, Administrative Procedures and Submittal Requirements in Downtown Zones. Department of Construction and Land Use, City of Seattle, July 15, 1985.

About the Authors

The authors are senior staff members of the Institute for Environmental Negotiation, which is affiliated with the Department of Urban and Environmental Planning of the School of Architecture at the University of Virginia, Charlottesville. The institute helps parties resolve environmental and development disputes through facilitation and mediation and assists communities in building consensus on various planning and growth management issues.

Preparation of *America's Downtowns* involved extensive collaboration among the authors. The resulting stories about each of the 10 cities represent the collective views of all three authors based on their visits, interviews and study of each city as well as their many years of experience dealing with issues related to cities, urban planning, conflict resolution and consensus building.

Richard C. Collins, founder and director of the Institute for Environmental Negotiation, is a professor of urban and environmental planning at the University of Virginia. He has served as a mediator in cases involving such matters as historic preservation and downtown development, groundwater protection, hazardous waste disposal and land development around the Chesapeake Bay. He has written numerous articles on land use, conflict resolution and related topics.

A. Bruce Dotson, assistant director of the institute, is an associate professor of urban and environmental planning at the university. Dotson has mediated a variety of disputes involving local land-use decisions, national forest management plans, groundwater and wetlands protection and related issues. He has contributed to several books on land-use planning and conflict resolution.

Elizabeth B. Waters, senior associate at the institute, has mediated conflicts involving neighborhoods, rural economic development, historic preservation, Chesapeake Bay water quality and related issues. Waters is a city council member and former mayor of Charlottesville and a member of Virginia's Commission on Population Growth and Development. She is a lecturer and has written articles and case studies on consensus building and conflict resolution.